RRANGED BY JEAN TAVENS GAN

FEATURING EXTRA LYRICS TO ALL THE SONGS — 12 PULL-OUT SETS

7777 W. BLUEMOUND RD. P.O. BOX 13819 MILWAUKEE, WI 53213

ANGELS FROM THE REALMS OF GLORY

3. Sages, leave your contemplations,
Brighter visions beam afar;
Seek the great Desire of nations,
Ye have seen his natal star.

Come and worship! Come and worship!
Worship Christ the newborn King!

4. All creation, join in praising
God, the Father, Spirit, Son,
Evermore your voices raising
To the eternal Three in One.

Come and worship! Come and worship!
Worship Christ the newborn King!

CAROL OF THE BELLS

Joyously
p cresc. poco a poco
2

N.C.
pp
cresc.
Hark to the bells, hark to the bells, tell - ing us all Je - sus is King!
2
Pedal:

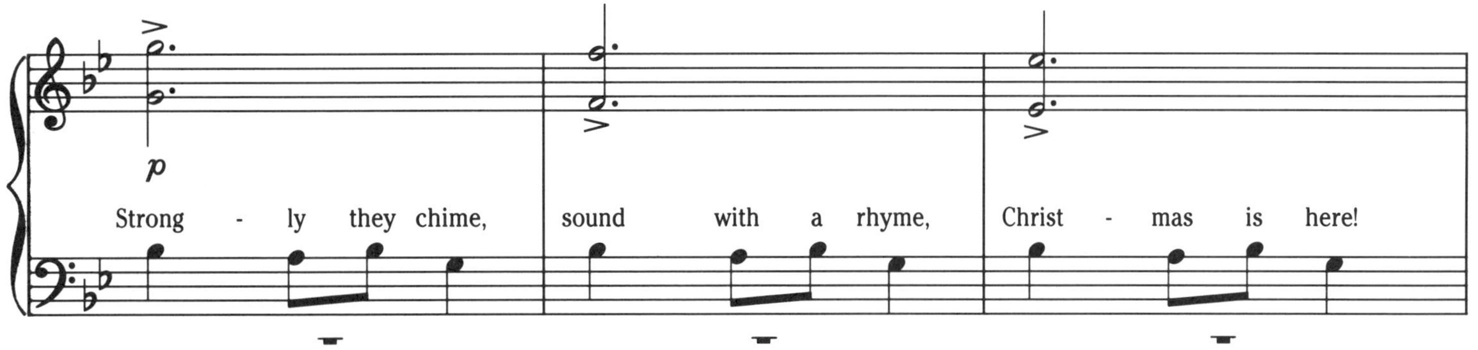
p
Strong - ly they chime, sound with a rhyme, Christ - mas is here!

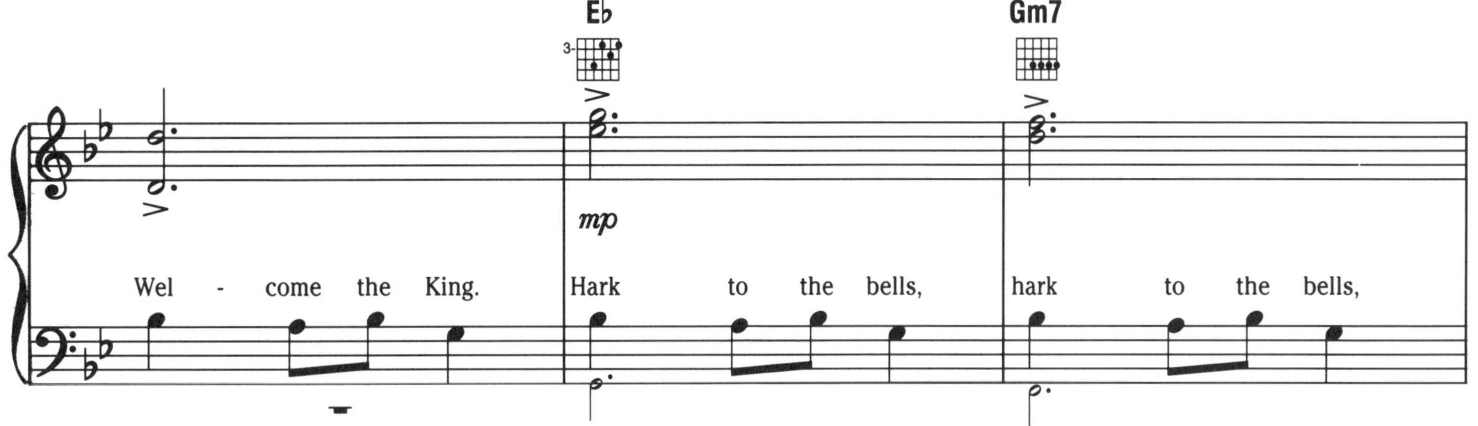
Eb
3-
Gm7
mp
Wel - come the King. Hark to the bells, hark to the bells,

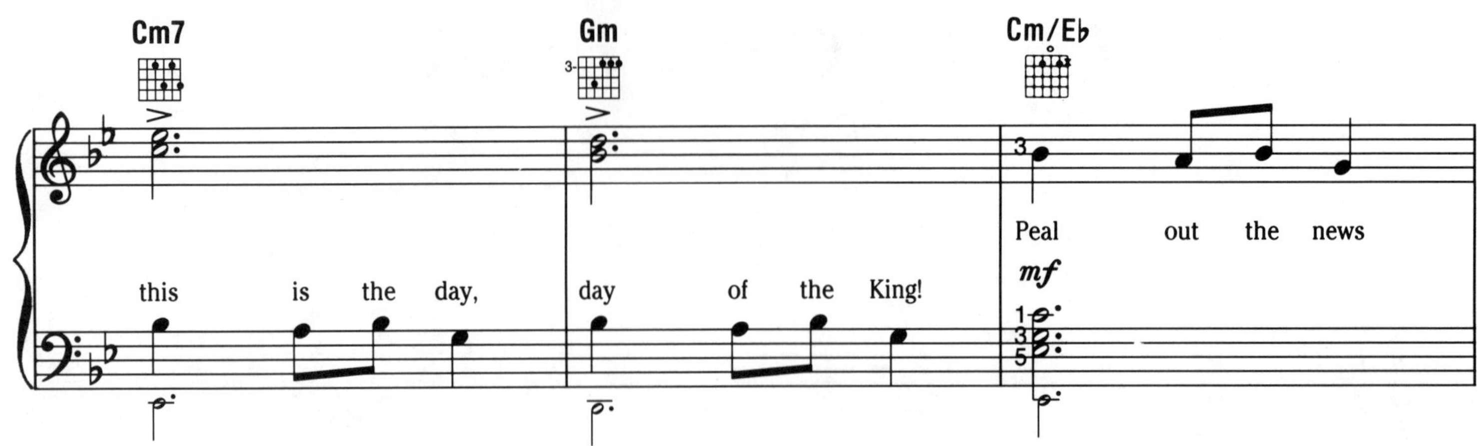
Cm7
Gm
Cm/E♭
Peal out the news
this is the day, day of the King!
mf

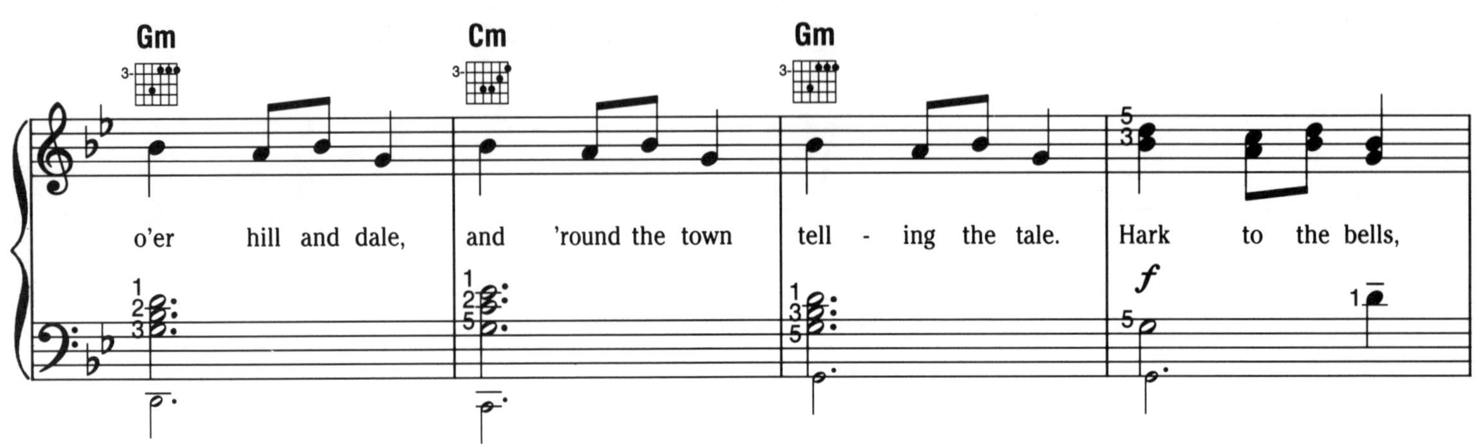
Gm
Cm
Gm
o'er hill and dale, and 'round the town tell - ing the tale. Hark to the bells,
f

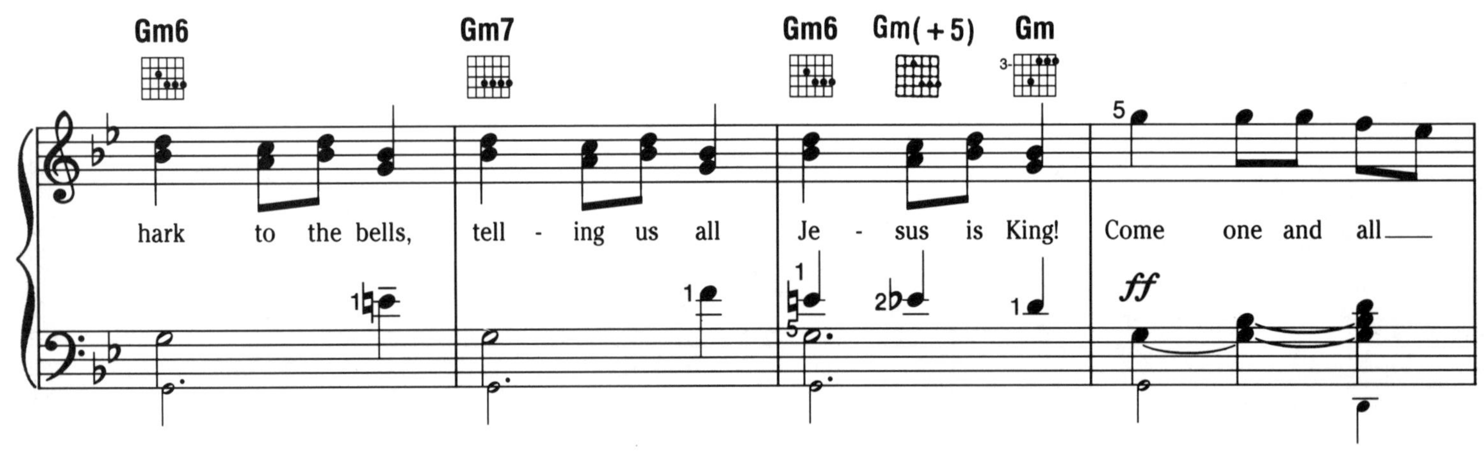
Gm6
Gm7
Gm6
Gm(+5)
Gm
hark to the bells, tell - ing us all Je - sus is King! Come one and all
ff

Cm
Gm
hap - pi - ly sing songs of good will, O let them sing!

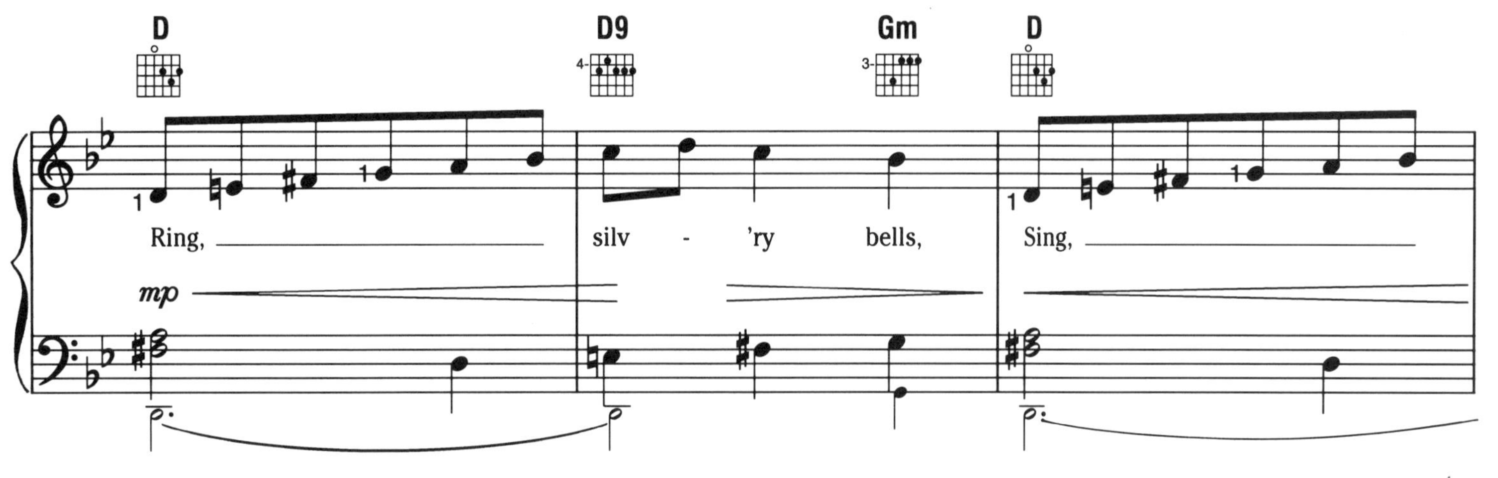
D
D9
Gm
D
Ring,
silv - 'ry bells,
Sing,
mp

D9
Gm
Cm7
joy - ous bells!
Strong - ly they chime,
sound with a rhyme,
mf

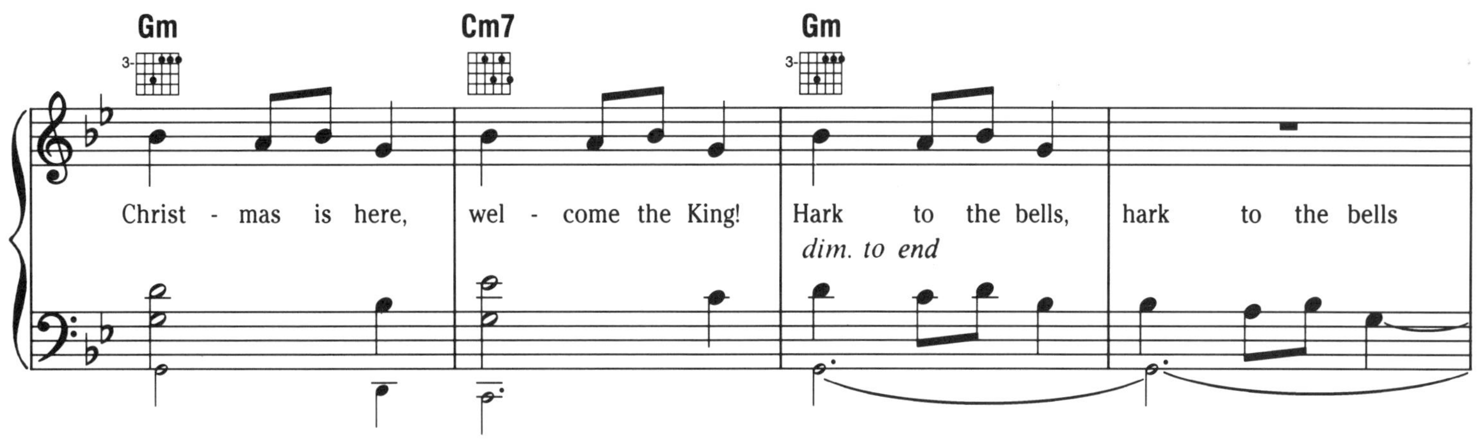
Gm
Cm7
Gm
Christ - mas is here,
wel - come the King!
Hark to the bells,
hark to the bells
dim. to end

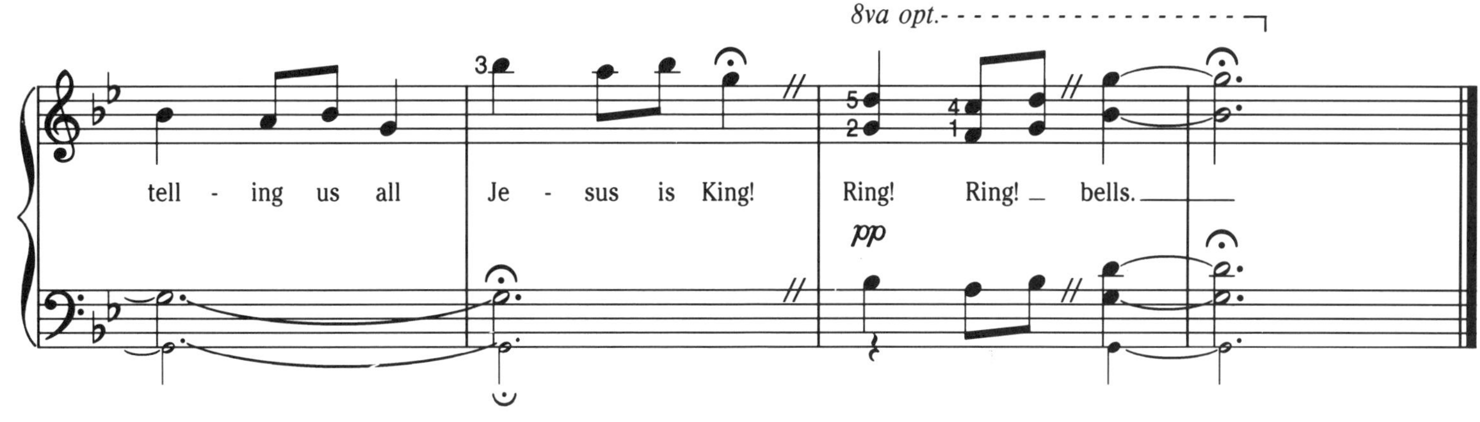
8va opt.
tell - ing us all
Je - sus is King!
Ring! Ring! bells.
pp

ANGELS WE HAVE HEARD ON HIGH

2. Shepherds, why this jubilee?
Why your joyous strains prolong?
What the gladsome tidings be
Which inspire your heavenly song?

Gloria in excelsis Deo,
Gloria in excelsis Deo.

3. Come to Bethlehem and see
Him whose birth the angels sing;
Come, adore on bended knee
Christ, the Lord, the new-born King.

Gloria in excelsis Deo,
Gloria in excelsis Deo.

4. See him in a manger laid
Whom the angels praise above;
Mary, Joseph, lend your aid,
While we raise our hearts in love.

Gloria in excelsis Deo,
Gloria in excelsis Deo.

AWAY IN A MANGER

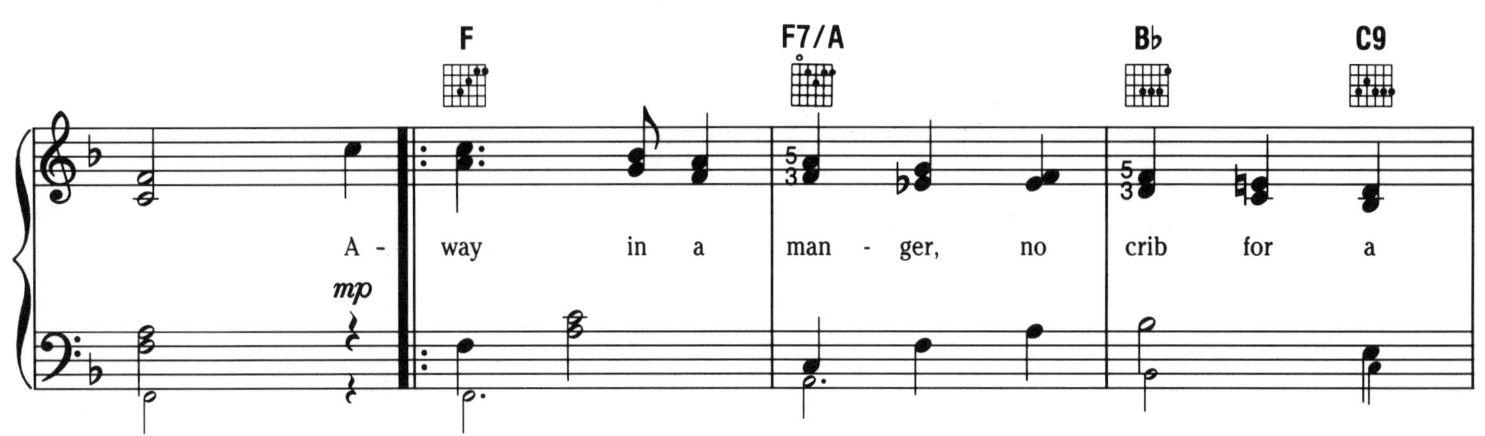

2. The cattle are lowing, the baby awakes,
But Little Lord Jesus, no crying He makes.
I love Thee, Lord Jesus, look down from the sky,
And stay by my cradle till morning is nigh.

3. Be near me, Lord Jesus; I ask Thee to stay
Close by me forever, and love me, I pray.
Bless all the dear children in Thy tender care,
And fit us for heaven, to live with Thee there.

COVENTRY CAROL

3. Herod the king, in his raging,
Charged he hath this day.
His men of might, in his own sight,
All young children to slay.

4. That woe is me, poor child for thee!
And ever morn and day,
For thy parting neither say nor sing
By by, lully lullay!

NOEL! NOEL!

Broadly
C Dm7 G7sus
f
Pedal:
G7 C G F C F G7 C G
No - el! No - el! Good news I tell, And
mp
Am G D7 G D7sus D G C G C G
eke a won - der sto - ry: A vir - gin mild
mf
C D G C F E Am F G7sus G7 C
borne a child, Je - sus the King of glo - ry.
f

THE FIRST NOEL

2. They looked up and saw a star
Shining in the East, beyond them far;
And to the earth it gave great light,
And so it continued both day and night.
Refrain

3. And by the light of that same star,
Three wise men came for country far;
To seek for a King was their intent,
And to follow the star wherever it went.
Refrain

4. This star drew night to the northwest,
O'er Bethlehem it took its rest;
And there it did both stop and stay,
Right over the place where Jesus lay.
Refrain

5. Then entered in those wise men three,
Full reverently upon their knee;
And offered there in His presence,
Their gold, and myrrh, and frankincense.
Refrain

GO TELL IT ON THE MOUNTAIN

Stately
f
Pedal:

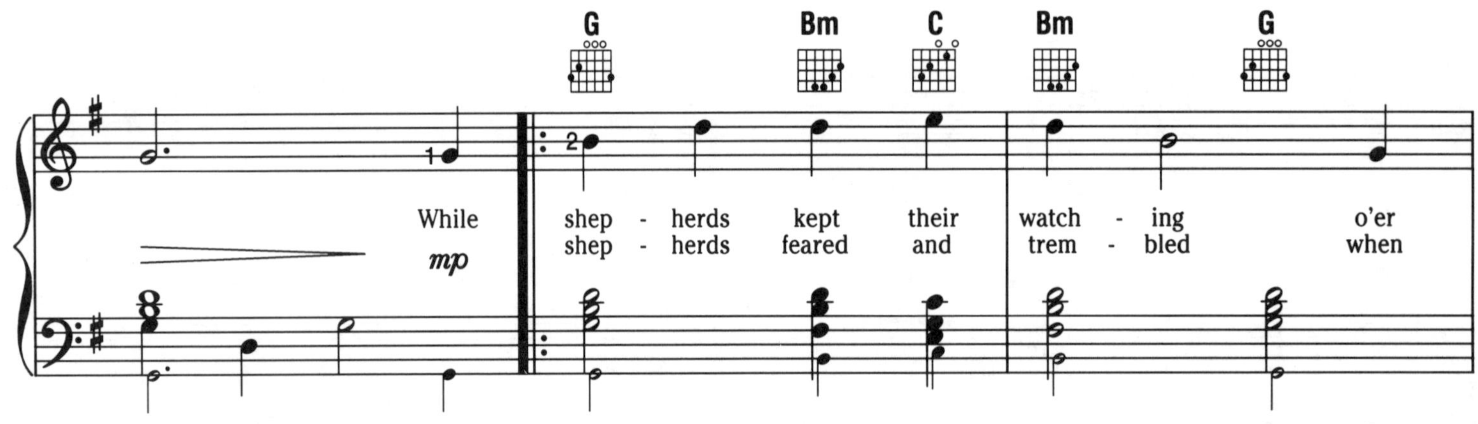
G
Bm
C
Bm
G
mp
While
shep - herds kept their watch - ing o'er
shep - herds feared and trem - bled when

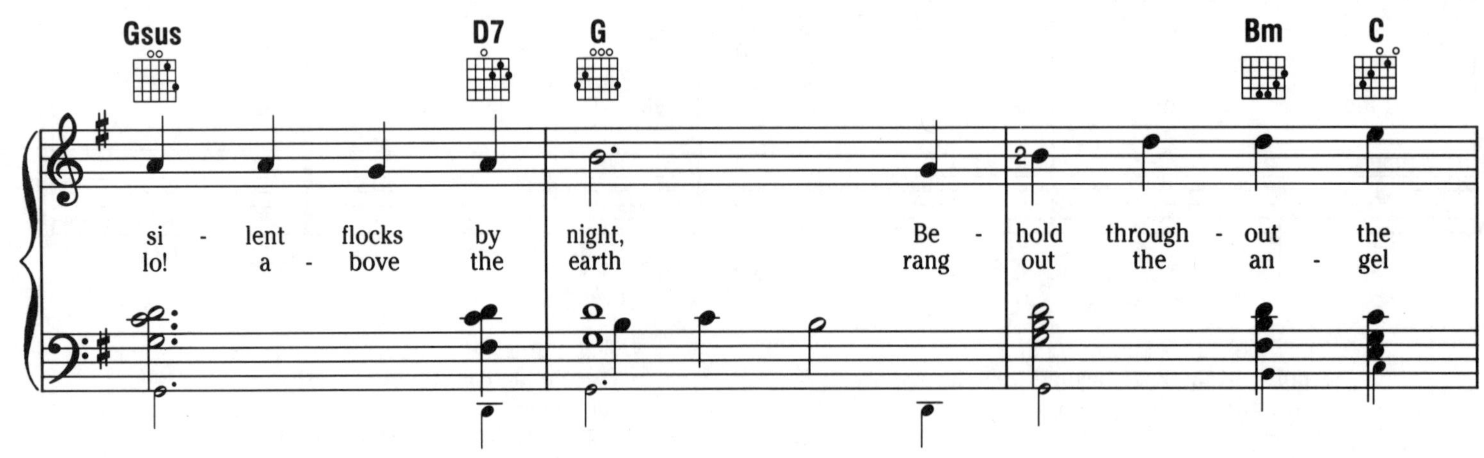
Gsus
D7
G
Bm
C
si - lent flocks by night, Be - hold through - out the
lo! a - bove the earth rang out the an - gel

G B7 Em Em7 A7 D7sus D7
heav - ens there shone a ho - ly light.
cho - rus that hailed our Sav - ior's birth.
Marcato
G C G Em Em7 D7 C D7
Go, tell it on the moun - tain, o - ver the hills and
G C G C G Em Em7
ev - 'ry - where, Go, tell it on the moun - tain that
Am D7 G C G G C G
Je - sus Christ is born. The born.

GOOD KING WENCESLAS

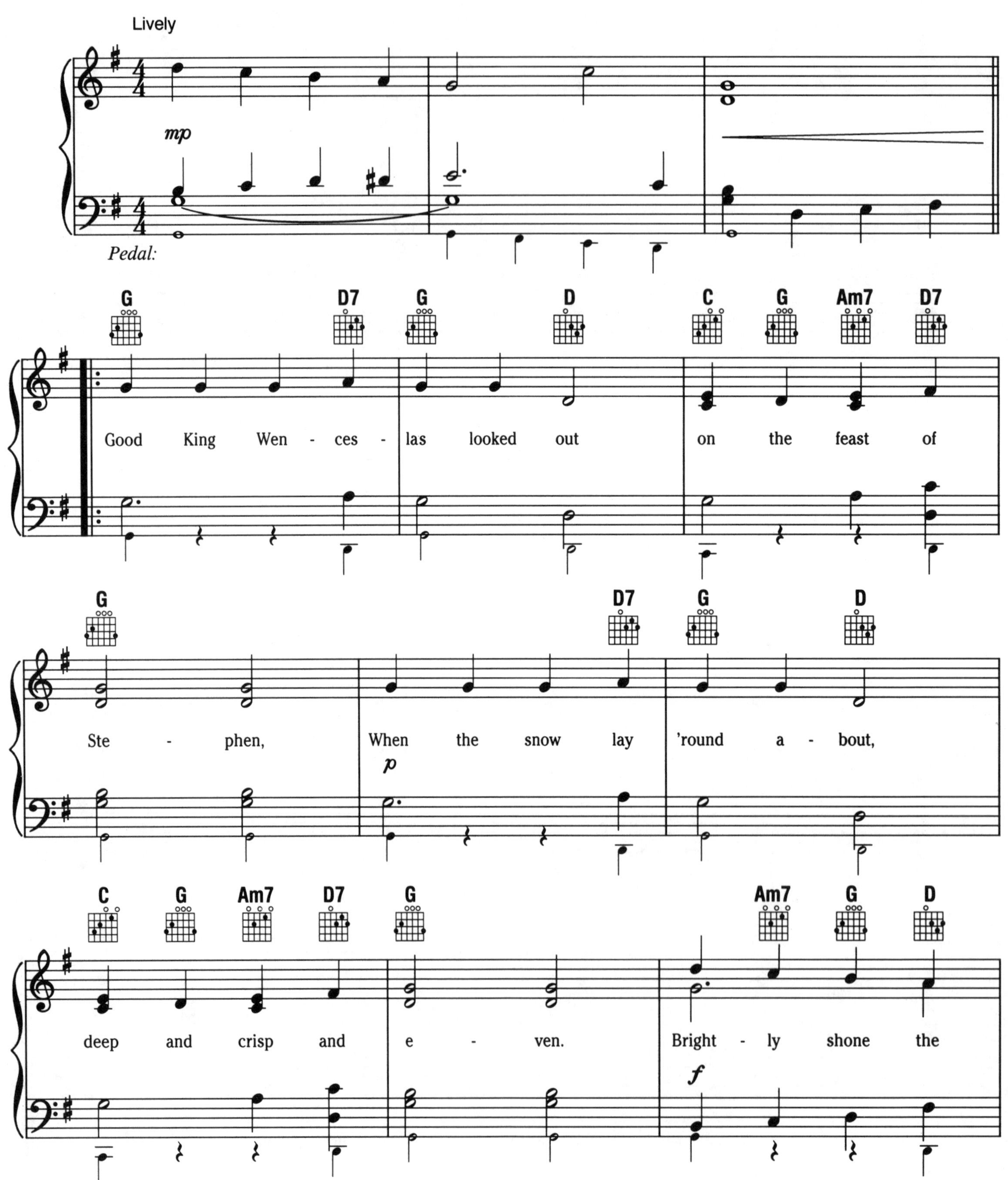

2. "Hither page, and stand by me,
   If thou know'st it, telling,
   Yonder peasant, who is he?
   Where and what his dwelling?"
   "Sire, he lives a good league hence,
   Underneath the mountain;
   Right against the forest fence,
   By Saint Agnes' fountain."

3. "Bring me flesh, and bring me wine,
   Bring me pine-logs hither;
   Thou and I will see him dine
   When we bear them thither."
   Page and monarch forth they went,
   Forth they went together;
   Through the rude winds wild lament:
   And the bitter weather.

4. "Sire, the night is darker now,
   And the wind blows stronger;
   Fails my heart, I know not how,
   I can go not longer."
   "Mark my footsteps, my good page,
   Tread thou in them boldly:
   Thou shalt find the winter's rage
   Freeze thy blood less coldly."

5. In his master's steps he trod,
   Where the snow lay dinted;
   Heat was in the very sod
   Which the saint had printed.
   Therefore, Christian men, be sure,
   Wealth or rank possessing,
   Ye who now will bless the poor,
   Shall yourselves find blessing.

JOY TO THE WORLD

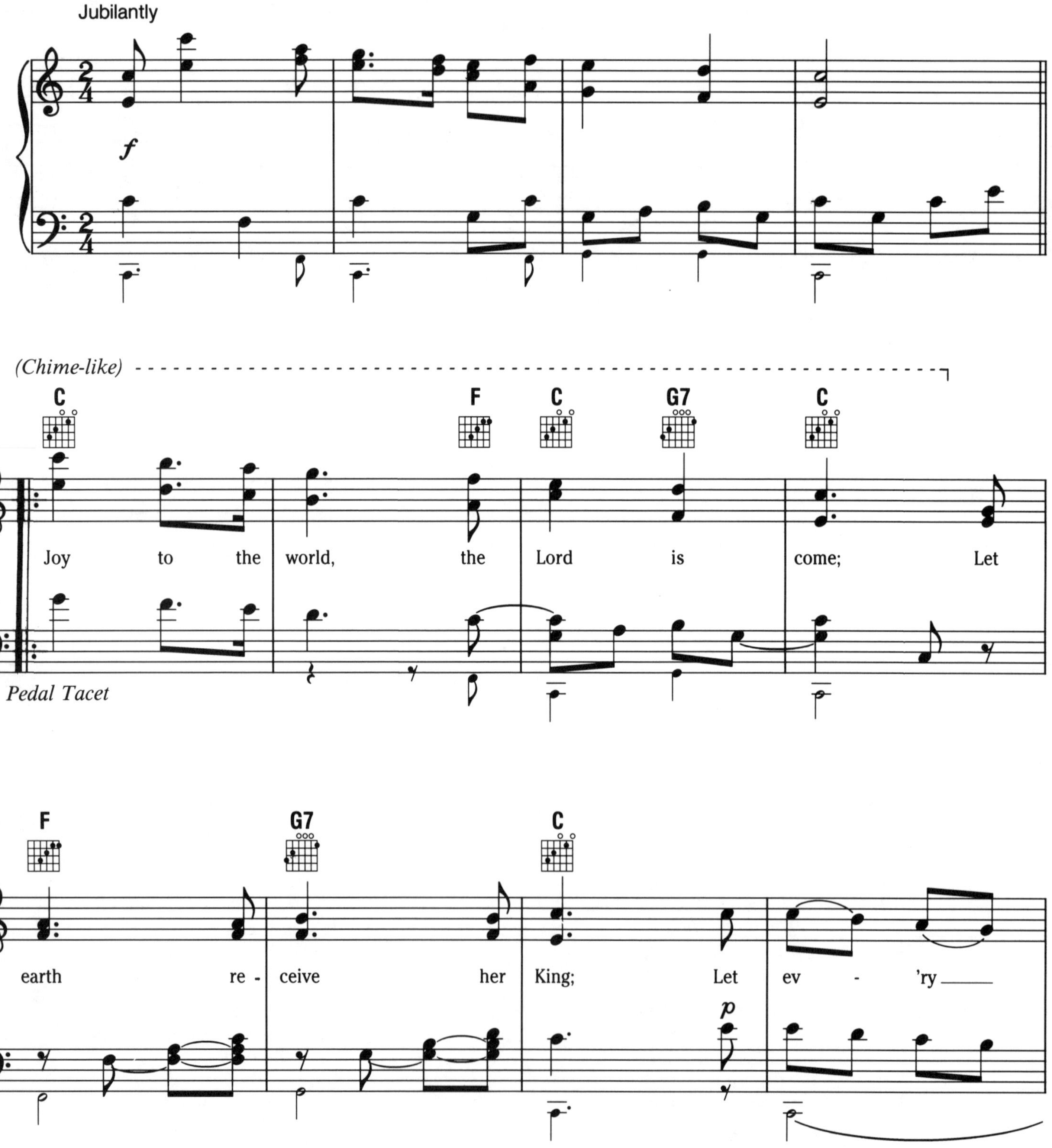

Jubilantly

f

(Chime-like)

C F C G7 C

Joy to the world, the Lord is come; Let

Pedal Tacet

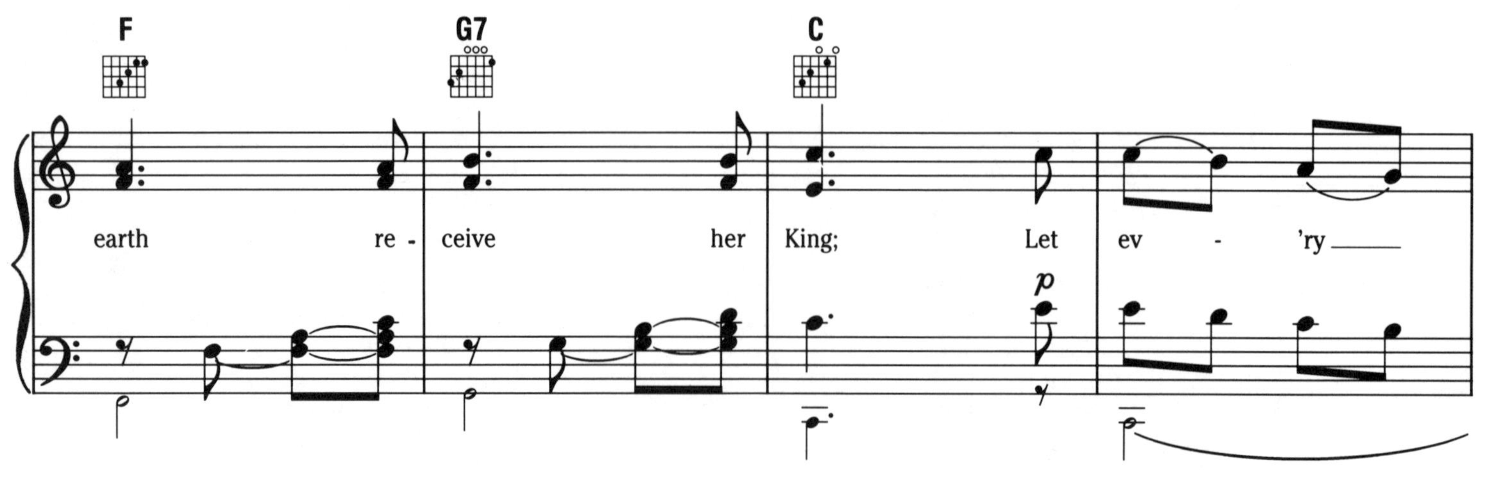

2. He rules the world with truth and grace,
And makes the nations prove
The glories of His righteousness,
And wonders of His love,
And wonders of His love,
And wonders, wonders of His love.

3. No more let sins and sorrows grow,
Nor thorns infest the ground;
He comes to make his blessings flow
Far as the curse is found.
Far as the curse is found
Far as far as the curse is found.

4. He rules the world with truth and grace,
And makes the nations prove
The glories of his righteousness,
And wonders of His love.
And wonders of His love
And wonders, wonders of His love.

HARK! THE HERALD ANGELS SING

Joyfully
f
Pedal:
F
C
F
C7
F
Hark! The her - ald an - gels sing, "Glo - ry to the new - born King!
mf
Dm
G7
C
G7
C
Peace on earth, and mer - cy mild, God and sin - ners re - con - ciled."
N.C.
C7
F
C7
N.C.
C7
F
C7
Joy - ful all ye na - tions rise, Join the tri - umph of the skies;
f

LYRICS FOR

Singalong Christmas Carols

ANGELS FROM THE REALMS OF GLORY

1. Angels from the realms of glory,
   Wing your flight o'er all the earth,
   Ye who sang creation's story,
   Now proclaim Messiah's birth.

   Come and worship! Come and worship!
   Worship Christ the newborn King!

2. Sages, leave your contemplations,
   Brighter visions beam afar,
   Seek the great Desire of nations
   Ye have seen His natal star.

   Come and worship! Come and worship!
   Worship Christ the newborn King!

3. Sages, leave your contemplations,
   Brighter visions beam afar;
   Seek the great Desire of nations,
   Ye have seen his natal star.

   Come and worship! Come and worship!
   Worship Christ the newborn King!

4. All creation, join in praising
   God, the Father, Spirit, Son,
   Evermore your voices raising
   To the eternal Three in One.

   Come and worship! Come and worship!
   Worship Christ the newborn King!

ANGELS WE HAVE HEARD ON HIGH

1. Angels we have heard on high
   Sweetly singing o'er the plains,
   And the mountains in reply
   Echoing their joyous strains.

   Gloria in excelsis Deo,
   Gloria in excelsis Deo.

2. Shepherds, why this jubilee?
   Why your joyous strains prolong?
   What the gladsome tidings be
   Which inspire your heavenly song?

   Gloria in excelsis Deo,
   Gloria in excelsis Deo.

3. Come to Bethlehem and see
   Him whose birth the angels sing;
   Come, adore on bended knee
   Christ, the Lord, the new-born King.

   Gloria in excelsis Deo,
   Gloria, in excelsis Deo.

4. See him in a manger laid
   Whom the angels praise above;
   Mary, Joseph, lend your aid,
   While we raise our hearts in love.

   Gloria in excelsis Deo,
   Gloria in excelsis Deo.

AWAY IN A MANGER

1. Away in a manger, no crib for a bed,
   The little Lord Jesus laid down His
   sweet head.
   The stars in the sky looked down
   where He lay,
   The little Lord Jesus, asleep on the hay.

2. The cattle are lowing, the baby awakes,
   But Little Lord Jesus, no crying
   He makes.
   I love Thee, Lord Jesus, look down from
   the sky,
   And stay by my cradle till morning
   is nigh.

3. Be near me, Lord Jesus; I ask Thee to stay
   Close by me forever, and love me, I pray.
   Bless all the dear children in Thy
   tender care,
   And fit us for heaven, to live with
   Thee there.

CAROL OF THE BELLS

Hark to the bells, hark to the bells,
Telling us all Jesus is King!
Strongly they chime, sound with
a rhyme,
Christmas is here! Welcome the King.
Hark to the bells, hark to the bells,
This is the day, day of the King!
Peal out the news oer hill and dale,
And 'round the town telling the tale.
Hark to the bells, hark to the bells,
Telling us all Jesus is King!

Come one and all happily sing
Songs of goodwill, o let them sing.

Ring, silv'ry bells, Sing, joyous bells!

Strongly they chime, sound with a rhyme,
Christmas is here, welcome the King!
Hark to the bells, hark to the bells,
Telling us all Jesus is King!

Ring! Ring! Bells.

COVENTRY CAROL

1. Lullay, thou little tiny child
   By by, lully, lullay.
   Lullay, thou little tiny child,
   By by, lully, lullay.

2. O sisters too, how may we do,
   For to preserve this day.
   This poor youngling for whome we sing.
   By by, lully, lullay.

3. Herod the king, in his raging,
   Charged he hath this day.
   His men of might, in his own sight,
   All young children to slay.

4. That woe is me, poor child for thee!
   And ever morn and day,
   For thy parting neither say nor sing
   By by, lully lullay!

THE FIRST NOEL

1. The first noel, the angel did say
   Was to certain poor shepherds in
   fields as they lay;
   In fields where they lay keeping
   their sheep,
   On a cold winter's night that was
   so deep.
   Refrain
   Noel, noel, noel, noel,
   Born is the King of Israel.

2. They looked up and saw a star
   Shining in the East, beyond them far;
   And to the earth it gave great light,
   And so it continued both day and night.
   Refrain

3. And by the light of that same star,
   Three wise men came for country far;
   To seek for a King was their intent,
   And to follow the star wherever it went
   Refrain

4. This star drew night to the northwest,
   O'er Bethlehem it took its rest;
   And there it did both stop and stay,
   Right over the place where Jesus lay.
   Refrain

5. Then entered in those wise men three,
   Full reverently upon their knee;
   And offered there in His presence,
   Their gold, and myrrh, and
   frankincense.
   Refrain

GO TELL IT ON THE MOUNTAIN

1. While shepherds kept their watching
O'er silent flocks by night,
Behold throughout the heavens
There shone a holy light.

Go, tell it on the mountain,
Over the hills and everywhere,
Go, tell it on the mountain
That Jesus Christ is born.

2. The shepherds feared and trembled
When lo! above the earth
Rang out the angel chorus
That hailed our Savior's birth.

Go, tell it on the mountain,
Over the hills and everywhere,
Go, tell it on the mountain
That Jesus Christ is born.

HARK! THE HERALD ANGELS SING

1. Hark! The herald angels sing,
"Glory to the newborn King!
Peace on earth, and mercy mild,
God and sinners reconciled."

Joyful all ye nations rise,
Join the triumph of the skies;
With th'angelic host proclaim,
"Christ is born in Bethlehem."

Hark! The herald angels sing,
"Glory to the newborn King!"

2. Christ, by highest heaven adored,
Christ, the everlasting Lord,
Late in time behold him come,
Offspring of a Virgin's womb.
Veiled in flesh the Godhead see;
Hail, the incarnate Deity,
Pleased as Man with man to dwell,
Jesus, our Immanuel!

Hark! The herald angels sing,
"Glory to the newborn King!"

3. Hail, the heaven-born Prince of Peace!
Hail, the Sun of Righteousness!
Light and life to all he brings,
Risen with healing in his wings.
Mild he lays his glory by,
Born that man no more may die,
Born to raise the sons of earth,
Born to give them second birth.

Hark! The herald angels sing,
"Glory to the newborn King!"

GOOD KING WENCESLAS

1. Good King Wenceslas looked out
On the feast of Stephen
When the snow lay 'round about,
Deep and crisp and even.
Brightly shown the moon that night,
Though the frost was cruel.
When a poor man came in sight,
Gathering winter fuel.

2. "Hither page, and stand by me,
If thou know'st it, telling,
Yonder peasant, who is he?
Where and what his dwelling?"
"Sire, he lives a good league hence,
Underneath the mountain;
Right against the forest fence,
By Saint Agnes' fountain."

3. "Bring me flesh, and bring me wine,
Bring me pine-logs hither;
Thou and I will see him dine
When we bear them thither."
Page and monarch forth they went,
Forth they went together;
Through the rude winds wild lament:
And the bitter weather.

4. "Sire, the night is darker now,
And the wind blows stronger;
Fails my heart, I know not how,
I can go not longer."
"Mark my footsteps, my good page,
Tread thou in them boldly:
Thou shalt find the winter's rage
Freeze thy blood less coldly."

5. In his master's steps he trod,
Where the snow lay dinted;
Heat was in the very sod
Which the saint had printed.
Therefore, Christian men, be sure,
Wealth or rank possessing,
Ye who now will bless the poor,
Shall yourselves find blessing.

IT CAME UPON THE MIDNIGHT CLEAR

1. It came upon the midnight clear,
That glorious song of old,
From angels bending near the earth
To touch their harps of gold.

Peace on the earth, good will to men
From heaven's all gracious King!

The world in solemn stillness lay
To hear the angels sing.

2. Still through the cloven they come,
With peaceful wings unfurled
And still their heavenly music floats
O'er all the weary world;
Above its sad and lowly plains
They bend on hovering wing,
And ever o'er its Babel sounds
The blessed angels sing.

3. Yet with the woes of sin and strife
The world hath suffered long;
Beneath the angel-strain have rolled
Two thousand years of wrong;
And man, at war with man, hears not
The love song which they bring:
O hush the noise, ye men of strife,
And hear the angels sing.

4. And ye, beneath life's crushing load,
Whose forms are bending low,
Who toil along the climbing way
With painful steps and slow:
Look now! for glad and golden hours
Come swiftly on the wing;
O rest beside the weary road,
And hear the angels sing.

5. For lo! the days are hastening on,
By prophet-bards foretold,
When, with the ever-circling years,
Shall come the Age of Gold;
When peace shall over all the earth
Its heavenly splendors fling,
And all the world give back the song
Which now the angels sing.

LYRICS FOR

Singalong Christmas Carols

ANGELS FROM THE REALMS OF GLORY

1. Angels from the realms of glory,
Wing your flight o'er all the earth,
Ye who sang creation's story,
Now proclaim Messiah's birth.

Come and worship! Come and worship!
Worship Christ the newborn King!

2. Sages, leave your contemplations,
Brighter visions beam afar,
Seek the great Desire of nations
Ye have seen His natal star.

Come and worship! Come and worship!
Worship Christ the newborn King!

3. Sages, leave your contemplations,
Brighter visions beam afar;
Seek the great Desire of nations,
Ye have seen his natal star.

Come and worship! Come and worship!
Worship Christ the newborn King!

4. All creation, join in praising
God, the Father, Spirit, Son,
Evermore your voices raising
To the eternal Three in One.

Come and worship! Come and worship!
Worship Christ the newborn King!

ANGELS WE HAVE HEARD ON HIGH

1. Angels we have heard on high
Sweetly singing o'er the plains,
And the mountains in reply
Echoing their joyous strains.

Gloria in excelsis Deo,
Gloria in excelsis Deo.

2. Shepherds, why this jubilee?
Why your joyous strains prolong?
What the gladsome tidings be
Which inspire your heavenly song?

Gloria in excelsis Deo,
Gloria in excelsis Deo.

3. Come to Bethlehem and see
Him whose birth the angels sing;
Come, adore on bended knee
Christ, the Lord, the new-born King.

Gloria in excelsis Deo,
Gloria, in excelsis Deo.

4. See him in a manger laid
Whom the angels praise above;
Mary, Joseph, lend your aid,
While we raise our hearts in love.

Gloria in excelsis Deo,
Gloria in excelsis Deo.

AWAY IN A MANGER

1. Away in a manger, no crib for a bed,
The little Lord Jesus laid down His
sweet head.
The stars in the sky looked down
where He lay,
The little Lord Jesus, asleep on the hay.

2. The cattle are lowing, the baby awakes,
But Little Lord Jesus, no crying
He makes.
I love Thee, Lord Jesus, look down from
the sky,
And stay by my cradle till morning
is nigh.

3. Be near me, Lord Jesus; I ask Thee to stay
Close by me forever, and love me, I pray.
Bless all the dear children in Thy
tender care,
And fit us for heaven, to live with
Thee there.

CAROL OF THE BELLS

Hark to the bells, hark to the bells,
Telling us all Jesus is King!
Strongly they chime, sound with
a rhyme,
Christmas is here! Welcome the King.
Hark to the bells, hark to the bells,
This is the day, day of the King!
Peal out the news oer hill and dale,
And 'round the town telling the tale.
Hark to the bells, hark to the bells,
Telling us all Jesus is King!

Come one and all happily sing
Songs of goodwill, o let them sing.

Ring, silv'ry bells, Sing, joyous bells!

Strongly they chime, sound with a rhyme,
Christmas is here, welcome the King!
Hark to the bells, hark to the bells,
Telling us all Jesus is King!

Ring! Ring! Bells.

COVENTRY CAROL

1. Lullay, thou little tiny child
By by, lully, lullay.
Lullay, thou little tiny child,
By by, lully, lullay.

2. O sisters too, how may we do,
For to preserve this day.
This poor youngling for whome we sing.
By by, lully, lullay.

3. Herod the king, in his raging,
Charged he hath this day.
His men of might, in his own sight,
All young children to slay.

4. That woe is me, poor child for thee!
And ever morn and day,
For thy parting neither say nor sing
By by, lully lullay!

THE FIRST NOEL

1. The first noel, the angel did say
Was to certain poor shepherds in
fields as they lay;
In fields where they lay keeping
their sheep,
On a cold winter's night that was
so deep.
Refrain
Noel, noel, noel, noel,
Born is the King of Israel.

2. They looked up and saw a star
Shining in the East, beyond them far;
And to the earth it gave great light,
And so it continued both day and night.
Refrain

3. And by the light of that same star,
Three wise men came for country far;
To seek for a King was their intent,
And to follow the star wherever it went
Refrain

4. This star drew night to the northwest,
O'er Bethlehem it took its rest;
And there it did both stop and stay,
Right over the place where Jesus lay.
Refrain

5. Then entered in those wise men three,
Full reverently upon their knee;
And offered there in His presence,
Their gold, and myrrh, and
frankincense.
Refrain

GO TELL IT ON THE MOUNTAIN

1. While shepherds kept their watching
   O'er silent flocks by night,
   Behold throughout the heavens
   There shone a holy light.

   Go, tell it on the mountain,
   Over the hills and everywhere,
   Go, tell it on the mountain
   That Jesus Christ is born.

2. The shepherds feared and trembled
   When lo! above the earth
   Rang out the angel chorus
   That hailed our Savior's birth.

   Go, tell it on the mountain,
   Over the hills and everywhere,
   Go, tell it on the mountain
   That Jesus Christ is born.

HARK! THE HERALD ANGELS SING

1. Hark! The herald angels sing,
   "Glory to the newborn King!
   Peace on earth, and mercy mild,
   God and sinners reconciled."

   Joyful all ye nations rise,
   Join the triumph of the skies;
   With th'angelic host proclaim,
   "Christ is born in Bethlehem."

   Hark! The herald angels sing,
   "Glory to the newborn King!"

2. Christ, by highest heaven adored,
   Christ, the everlasting Lord,
   Late in time behold him come,
   Offspring of a Virgin's womb.
   Veiled in flesh the Godhead see;
   Hail, the incarnate Deity,
   Pleased as Man with man to dwell,
   Jesus, our Immanuel!

   Hark! The herald angels sing,
   "Glory to the newborn King!"

3. Hail, the heaven-born Prince of Peace!
   Hail, the Sun of Righteousness!
   Light and life to all he brings,
   Risen with healing in his wings.
   Mild he lays his glory by,
   Born that man no more may die,
   Born to raise the sons of earth,
   Born to give them second birth.

   Hark! The herald angels sing,
   "Glory to the newborn King!"

GOOD KING WENCESLAS

1. Good King Wenceslas looked out
   On the feast of Stephen
   When the snow lay 'round about,
   Deep and crisp and even.
   Brightly shown the moon that night,
   Though the frost was cruel.
   When a poor man came in sight,
   Gathering winter fuel.

2. "Hither page, and stand by me,
   If thou know'st it, telling,
   Yonder peasant, who is he?
   Where and what his dwelling?"
   "Sire, he lives a good league hence,
   Underneath the mountain;
   Right against the forest fence,
   By Saint Agnes' fountain."

3. "Bring me flesh, and bring me wine,
   Bring me pine-logs hither;
   Thou and I will see him dine
   When we bear them thither."
   Page and monarch forth they went,
   Forth they went together;
   Through the rude winds wild lament:
   And the bitter weather.

4. "Sire, the night is darker now,
   And the wind blows stronger;
   Fails my heart, I know not how,
   I can go not longer."
   "Mark my footsteps, my good page,
   Tread thou in them boldly:
   Thou shalt find the winter's rage
   Freeze thy blood less coldly."

5. In his master's steps he trod,
   Where the snow lay dinted;
   Heat was in the very sod
   Which the saint had printed.
   Therefore, Christian men, be sure,
   Wealth or rank possessing,
   Ye who now will bless the poor,
   Shall yourselves find blessing.

IT CAME UPON THE MIDNIGHT CLEAR

1. It came upon the midnight clear,
   That glorious song of old,
   From angels bending near the earth
   To touch their harps of gold.

   Peace on the earth, good will to men
   From heaven's all gracious King!

   The world in solemn stillness lay
   To hear the angels sing.

2. Still through the cloven they come,
   With peaceful wings unfurled
   And still their heavenly music floats
   O'er all the weary world;
   Above its sad and lowly plains
   They bend on hovering wing,
   And ever o'er its Babel sounds
   The blessed angels sing.

3. Yet with the woes of sin and strife
   The world hath suffered long;
   Beneath the angel-strain have rolled
   Two thousand years of wrong;
   And man, at war with man, hears not
   The love song which they bring:
   O hush the noise, ye men of strife,
   And hear the angels sing.

4. And ye, beneath life's crushing load,
   Whose forms are bending low,
   Who toil along the climbing way
   With painful steps and slow:
   Look now! for glad and golden hours
   Come swiftly on the wing;
   O rest beside the weary road,
   And hear the angels sing.

5. For lo! the days are hastening on,
   By prophet-bards foretold,
   When, with the ever-circling years,
   Shall come the Age of Gold;
   When peace shall over all the earth
   Its heavenly splendors fling,
   And all the world give back the song
   Which now the angels sing.

LYRICS FOR

Singalong Christmas Carols

ANGELS FROM THE REALMS OF GLORY

1. Angels from the realms of glory,
   Wing your flight o'er all the earth,
   Ye who sang creation's story,
   Now proclaim Messiah's birth.

   Come and worship! Come and worship!
   Worship Christ the newborn King!

2. Sages, leave your contemplations,
   Brighter visions beam afar,
   Seek the great Desire of nations
   Ye have seen His natal star.

   Come and worship! Come and worship!
   Worship Christ the newborn King!

3. Sages, leave your contemplations,
   Brighter visions beam afar;
   Seek the great Desire of nations,
   Ye have seen his natal star.

   Come and worship! Come and worship!
   Worship Christ the newborn King!

4. All creation, join in praising
   God, the Father, Spirit, Son,
   Evermore your voices raising
   To the eternal Three in One.

   Come and worship! Come and worship!
   Worship Christ the newborn King!

ANGELS WE HAVE HEARD ON HIGH

1. Angels we have heard on high
   Sweetly singing o'er the plains,
   And the mountains in reply
   Echoing their joyous strains.

   Gloria in excelsis Deo,
   Gloria in excelsis Deo.

2. Shepherds, why this jubilee?
   Why your joyous strains prolong?
   What the gladsome tidings be
   Which inspire your heavenly song?

   Gloria in excelsis Deo,
   Gloria in excelsis Deo.

3. Come to Bethlehem and see
   Him whose birth the angels sing;
   Come, adore on bended knee
   Christ, the Lord, the new-born King.

   Gloria in excelsis Deo,
   Gloria, in excelsis Deo.

4. See him in a manger laid
   Whom the angels praise above;
   Mary, Joseph, lend your aid,
   While we raise our hearts in love.

   Gloria in excelsis Deo,
   Gloria in excelsis Deo.

AWAY IN A MANGER

1. Away in a manger, no crib for a bed,
   The little Lord Jesus laid down His
   sweet head.
   The stars in the sky looked down
   where He lay,
   The little Lord Jesus, asleep on the hay.

2. The cattle are lowing, the baby awakes,
   But Little Lord Jesus, no crying
   He makes.
   I love Thee, Lord Jesus, look down from
   the sky,
   And stay by my cradle till morning
   is nigh.

3. Be near me, Lord Jesus; I ask Thee to stay
   Close by me forever, and love me, I pray.
   Bless all the dear children in Thy
   tender care,
   And fit us for heaven, to live with
   Thee there.

CAROL OF THE BELLS

Hark to the bells, hark to the bells,
Telling us all Jesus is King!
Strongly they chime, sound with
a rhyme,
Christmas is here! Welcome the King.
Hark to the bells, hark to the bells,
This is the day, day of the King!
Peal out the news oer hill and dale,
And 'round the town telling the tale.
Hark to the bells, hark to the bells,
Telling us all Jesus is King!

Come one and all happily sing
Songs of goodwill, o let them sing.

Ring, silv'ry bells, Sing, joyous bells!

Strongly they chime, sound with a rhyme,
Christmas is here, welcome the King!
Hark to the bells, hark to the bells,
Telling us all Jesus is King!

Ring! Ring! Bells.

COVENTRY CAROL

1. Lullay, thou little tiny child
   By by, lully, lullay.
   Lullay, thou little tiny child,
   By by, lully, lullay.

2. O sisters too, how may we do,
   For to preserve this day.
   This poor youngling for whome we sing.
   By by, lully, lullay.

3. Herod the king, in his raging,
   Charged he hath this day.
   His men of might, in his own sight,
   All young children to slay.

4. That woe is me, poor child for thee!
   And ever morn and day,
   For thy parting neither say nor sing
   By by, lully lullay!

THE FIRST NOEL

1. The first noel, the angel did say
   Was to certain poor shepherds in
   fields as they lay;
   In fields where they lay keeping
   their sheep,
   On a cold winter's night that was
   so deep.
   Refrain
   Noel, noel, noel, noel,
   Born is the King of Israel.

2. They looked up and saw a star
   Shining in the East, beyond them far;
   And to the earth it gave great light,
   And so it continued both day and night.
   Refrain

3. And by the light of that same star,
   Three wise men came for country far;
   To seek for a King was their intent,
   And to follow the star wherever it went
   Refrain

4. This star drew night to the northwest,
   O'er Bethlehem it took its rest;
   And there it did both stop and stay,
   Right over the place where Jesus lay.
   Refrain

5. Then entered in those wise men three,
   Full reverently upon their knee;
   And offered there in His presence,
   Their gold, and myrrh, and
   frankincense.
   Refrain

GO TELL IT ON THE MOUNTAIN

1. While shepherds kept their watching
   O'er silent flocks by night,
   Behold throughout the heavens
   There shone a holy light.

   Go, tell it on the mountain,
   Over the hills and everywhere,
   Go, tell it on the mountain
   That Jesus Christ is born.

2. The shepherds feared and trembled
   When lo! above the earth
   Rang out the angel chorus
   That hailed our Savior's birth.

   Go, tell it on the mountain,
   Over the hills and everywhere,
   Go, tell it on the mountain
   That Jesus Christ is born.

HARK! THE HERALD ANGELS SING

1. Hark! The herald angels sing,
   "Glory to the newborn King!
   Peace on earth, and mercy mild,
   God and sinners reconciled."

   Joyful all ye nations rise,
   Join the triumph of the skies;
   With th'angelic host proclaim,
   "Christ is born in Bethlehem."

   Hark! The herald angels sing,
   "Glory to the newborn King!"

2. Christ, by highest heaven adored,
   Christ, the everlasting Lord,
   Late in time behold him come,
   Offspring of a Virgin's womb.
   Veiled in flesh the Godhead see;
   Hail, the incarnate Deity,
   Pleased as Man with man to dwell,
   Jesus, our Immanuel!

   Hark! The herald angels sing,
   "Glory to the newborn King!"

3. Hail, the heaven-born Prince of Peace!
   Hail, the Sun of Righteousness!
   Light and life to all he brings,
   Risen with healing in his wings.
   Mild he lays his glory by,
   Born that man no more may die,
   Born to raise the sons of earth,
   Born to give them second birth.

   Hark! The herald angels sing,
   "Glory to the newborn King!"

GOOD KING WENCESLAS

1. Good King Wenceslas looked out
   On the feast of Stephen
   When the snow lay 'round about,
   Deep and crisp and even.
   Brightly shown the moon that night,
   Though the frost was cruel.
   When a poor man came in sight,
   Gathering winter fuel.

2. "Hither page, and stand by me,
   If thou know'st it, telling,
   Yonder peasant, who is he?
   Where and what his dwelling?"
   "Sire, he lives a good league hence,
   Underneath the mountain;
   Right against the forest fence,
   By Saint Agnes' fountain."

3. "Bring me flesh, and bring me wine,
   Bring me pine-logs hither;
   Thou and I will see him dine
   When we bear them thither."
   Page and monarch forth they went,
   Forth they went together;
   Through the rude winds wild lament:
   And the bitter weather.

4. "Sire, the night is darker now,
   And the wind blows stronger;
   Fails my heart, I know not how,
   I can go not longer."
   "Mark my footsteps, my good page,
   Tread thou in them boldly:
   Thou shalt find the winter's rage
   Freeze thy blood less coldly."

5. In his master's steps he trod,
   Where the snow lay dinted;
   Heat was in the very sod
   Which the saint had printed.
   Therefore, Christian men, be sure,
   Wealth or rank possessing,
   Ye who now will bless the poor,
   Shall yourselves find blessing.

IT CAME UPON THE MIDNIGHT CLEAR

1. It came upon the midnight clear,
   That glorious song of old,
   From angels bending near the earth
   To touch their harps of gold.

   Peace on the earth, good will to men
   From heaven's all gracious King!

   The world in solemn stillness lay
   To hear the angels sing.

2. Still through the cloven they come,
   With peaceful wings unfurled
   And still their heavenly music floats
   O'er all the weary world;
   Above its sad and lowly plains
   They bend on hovering wing,
   And ever o'er its Babel sounds
   The blessed angels sing.

3. Yet with the woes of sin and strife
   The world hath suffered long;
   Beneath the angel-strain have rolled
   Two thousand years of wrong;
   And man, at war with man, hears not
   The love song which they bring:
   O hush the noise, ye men of strife,
   And hear the angels sing.

4. And ye, beneath life's crushing load,
   Whose forms are bending low,
   Who toil along the climbing way
   With painful steps and slow:
   Look now! for glad and golden hours
   Come swiftly on the wing;
   O rest beside the weary road,
   And hear the angels sing.

5. For lo! the days are hastening on,
   By prophet-bards foretold,
   When, with the ever-circling years,
   Shall come the Age of Gold;
   When peace shall over all the earth
   Its heavenly splendors fling,
   And all the world give back the song
   Which now the angels sing.

LYRICS FOR

Singalong Christmas Carols

ANGELS FROM THE REALMS OF GLORY

1. Angels from the realms of glory,
Wing your flight o'er all the earth,
Ye who sang creation's story,
Now proclaim Messiah's birth.

Come and worship! Come and worship!
Worship Christ the newborn King!

2. Sages, leave your contemplations,
Brighter visions beam afar,
Seek the great Desire of nations
Ye have seen His natal star.

Come and worship! Come and worship!
Worship Christ the newborn King!

3. Sages, leave your contemplations,
Brighter visions beam afar;
Seek the great Desire of nations,
Ye have seen his natal star.

Come and worship! Come and worship!
Worship Christ the newborn King!

4. All creation, join in praising
God, the Father, Spirit, Son,
Evermore your voices raising
To the eternal Three in One.

Come and worship! Come and worship!
Worship Christ the newborn King!

ANGELS WE HAVE HEARD ON HIGH

1. Angels we have heard on high
Sweetly singing o'er the plains,
And the mountains in reply
Echoing their joyous strains.

Gloria in excelsis Deo,
Gloria in excelsis Deo.

2. Shepherds, why this jubilee?
Why your joyous strains prolong?
What the gladsome tidings be
Which inspire your heavenly song?

Gloria in excelsis Deo,
Gloria in excelsis Deo.

3. Come to Bethlehem and see
Him whose birth the angels sing;
Come, adore on bended knee
Christ, the Lord, the new-born King.

Gloria in excelsis Deo,
Gloria, in excelsis Deo.

4. See him in a manger laid
Whom the angels praise above;
Mary, Joseph, lend your aid,
While we raise our hearts in love.

Gloria in excelsis Deo,
Gloria in excelsis Deo.

AWAY IN A MANGER

1. Away in a manger, no crib for a bed,
The little Lord Jesus laid down His
sweet head.
The stars in the sky looked down
where He lay,
The little Lord Jesus, asleep on the hay.

2. The cattle are lowing, the baby awakes,
But Little Lord Jesus, no crying
He makes.
I love Thee, Lord Jesus, look down from
the sky,
And stay by my cradle till morning
is nigh.

3. Be near me, Lord Jesus; I ask Thee to stay
Close by me forever, and love me, I pray.
Bless all the dear children in Thy
tender care,
And fit us for heaven, to live with
Thee there.

CAROL OF THE BELLS

Hark to the bells, hark to the bells,
Telling us all Jesus is King!
Strongly they chime, sound with
a rhyme,
Christmas is here! Welcome the King.
Hark to the bells, hark to the bells,
This is the day, day of the King!
Peal out the news oer hill and dale,
And 'round the town telling the tale.
Hark to the bells, hark to the bells,
Telling us all Jesus is King!

Come one and all happily sing
Songs of goodwill, o let them sing.

Ring, silv'ry bells, Sing, joyous bells!

Strongly they chime, sound with a rhyme,
Christmas is here, welcome the King!
Hark to the bells, hark to the bells,
Telling us all Jesus is King!

Ring! Ring! Bells.

COVENTRY CAROL

1. Lullay, thou little tiny child
By by, lully, lullay.
Lullay, thou little tiny child,
By by, lully, lullay.

2. O sisters too, how may we do,
For to preserve this day.
This poor youngling for whome we sing.
By by, lully, lullay.

3. Herod the king, in his raging,
Charged he hath this day.
His men of might, in his own sight,
All young children to slay.

4. That woe is me, poor child for thee!
And ever morn and day,
For thy parting neither say nor sing
By by, lully lullay!

THE FIRST NOEL

1. The first noel, the angel did say
Was to certain poor shepherds in
fields as they lay;
In fields where they lay keeping
their sheep,
On a cold winter's night that was
so deep.
Refrain
Noel, noel, noel, noel,
Born is the King of Israel.

2. They looked up and saw a star
Shining in the East, beyond them far;
And to the earth it gave great light,
And so it continued both day and night.
Refrain

3. And by the light of that same star,
Three wise men came for country far;
To seek for a King was their intent,
And to follow the star wherever it went
Refrain

4. This star drew night to the northwest,
O'er Bethlehem it took its rest;
And there it did both stop and stay,
Right over the place where Jesus lay.
Refrain

5. Then entered in those wise men three,
Full reverently upon their knee;
And offered there in His presence,
Their gold, and myrrh, and
frankincense.
Refrain

GO TELL IT ON THE MOUNTAIN

1. While shepherds kept their watching
O'er silent flocks by night,
Behold throughout the heavens
There shone a holy light.

Go, tell it on the mountain,
Over the hills and everywhere,
Go, tell it on the mountain
That Jesus Christ is born.

2. The shepherds feared and trembled
When lo! above the earth
Rang out the angel chorus
That hailed our Savior's birth.

Go, tell it on the mountain,
Over the hills and everywhere,
Go, tell it on the mountain
That Jesus Christ is born.

HARK! THE HERALD ANGELS SING

1. Hark! The herald angels sing,
"Glory to the newborn King!
Peace on earth, and mercy mild,
God and sinners reconciled."

Joyful all ye nations rise,
Join the triumph of the skies;
With th'angelic host proclaim,
"Christ is born in Bethlehem."

Hark! The herald angels sing,
"Glory to the newborn King!"

2. Christ, by highest heaven adored,
Christ, the everlasting Lord,
Late in time behold him come,
Offspring of a Virgin's womb.
Veiled in flesh the Godhead see;
Hail, the incarnate Deity,
Pleased as Man with man to dwell,
Jesus, our Immanuel!

Hark! The herald angels sing,
"Glory to the newborn King!"

3. Hail, the heaven-born Prince of Peace!
Hail, the Sun of Righteousness!
Light and life to all he brings,
Risen with healing in his wings.
Mild he lays his glory by,
Born that man no more may die,
Born to raise the sons of earth,
Born to give them second birth.

Hark! The herald angels sing,
"Glory to the newborn King!"

GOOD KING WENCESLAS

1. Good King Wenceslas looked out
On the feast of Stephen
When the snow lay 'round about,
Deep and crisp and even.
Brightly shown the moon that night,
Though the frost was cruel.
When a poor man came in sight,
Gathering winter fuel.

2. "Hither page, and stand by me,
If thou know'st it, telling,
Yonder peasant, who is he?
Where and what his dwelling?"
"Sire, he lives a good league hence,
Underneath the mountain;
Right against the forest fence,
By Saint Agnes' fountain."

3. "Bring me flesh, and bring me wine,
Bring me pine-logs hither;
Thou and I will see him dine
When we bear them thither."
Page and monarch forth they went,
Forth they went together;
Through the rude winds wild lament:
And the bitter weather.

4. "Sire, the night is darker now,
And the wind blows stronger;
Fails my heart, I know not how,
I can go not longer."
"Mark my footsteps, my good page,
Tread thou in them boldly:
Thou shalt find the winter's rage
Freeze thy blood less coldly."

5. In his master's steps he trod,
Where the snow lay dinted;
Heat was in the very sod
Which the saint had printed.
Therefore, Christian men, be sure,
Wealth or rank possessing,
Ye who now will bless the poor,
Shall yourselves find blessing.

IT CAME UPON THE MIDNIGHT CLEAR

1. It came upon the midnight clear,
That glorious song of old,
From angels bending near the earth
To touch their harps of gold.

Peace on the earth, good will to men
From heaven's all gracious King!

The world in solemn stillness lay
To hear the angels sing.

2. Still through the cloven they come,
With peaceful wings unfurled
And still their heavenly music floats
O'er all the weary world;
Above its sad and lowly plains
They bend on hovering wing,
And ever o'er its Babel sounds
The blessed angels sing.

3. Yet with the woes of sin and strife
The world hath suffered long;
Beneath the angel-strain have rolled
Two thousand years of wrong;
And man, at war with man, hears not
The love song which they bring:
O hush the noise, ye men of strife,
And hear the angels sing.

4. And ye, beneath life's crushing load,
Whose forms are bending low,
Who toil along the climbing way
With painful steps and slow:
Look now! for glad and golden hours
Come swiftly on the wing;
O rest beside the weary road,
And hear the angels sing.

5. For lo! the days are hastening on,
By prophet-bards foretold,
When, with the ever-circling years,
Shall come the Age of Gold;
When peace shall over all the earth
Its heavenly splendors fling,
And all the world give back the song
Which now the angels sing.

LYRICS FOR
Singalong Christmas Carols

ANGELS FROM THE REALMS OF GLORY

1. Angels from the realms of glory,
Wing your flight o'er all the earth,
Ye who sang creation's story,
Now proclaim Messiah's birth.

Come and worship! Come and worship!
Worship Christ the newborn King!

2. Sages, leave your contemplations,
Brighter visions beam afar,
Seek the great Desire of nations
Ye have seen His natal star.

Come and worship! Come and worship!
Worship Christ the newborn King!

3. Sages, leave your contemplations,
Brighter visions beam afar;
Seek the great Desire of nations,
Ye have seen his natal star.

Come and worship! Come and worship!
Worship Christ the newborn King!

4. All creation, join in praising
God, the Father, Spirit, Son,
Evermore your voices raising
To the eternal Three in One.

Come and worship! Come and worship!
Worship Christ the newborn King!

ANGELS WE HAVE HEARD ON HIGH

1. Angels we have heard on high
Sweetly singing o'er the plains,
And the mountains in reply
Echoing their joyous strains.

Gloria in excelsis Deo,
Gloria in excelsis Deo.

2. Shepherds, why this jubilee?
Why your joyous strains prolong?
What the gladsome tidings be
Which inspire your heavenly song?

Gloria in excelsis Deo,
Gloria in excelsis Deo.

3. Come to Bethlehem and see
Him whose birth the angels sing;
Come, adore on bended knee
Christ, the Lord, the new-born King.

Gloria in excelsis Deo,
Gloria, in excelsis Deo.

4. See him in a manger laid
Whom the angels praise above;
Mary, Joseph, lend your aid,
While we raise our hearts in love.

Gloria in excelsis Deo,
Gloria in excelsis Deo.

AWAY IN A MANGER

1. Away in a manger, no crib for a bed,
The little Lord Jesus laid down His sweet head.
The stars in the sky looked down where He lay,
The little Lord Jesus, asleep on the hay.

2. The cattle are lowing, the baby awakes,
But Little Lord Jesus, no crying He makes.
I love Thee, Lord Jesus, look down from the sky,
And stay by my cradle till morning is nigh.

3. Be near me, Lord Jesus; I ask Thee to stay
Close by me forever, and love me, I pray.
Bless all the dear children in Thy tender care,
And fit us for heaven, to live with Thee there.

CAROL OF THE BELLS

Hark to the bells, hark to the bells,
Telling us all Jesus is King!
Strongly they chime, sound with a rhyme,
Christmas is here! Welcome the King.
Hark to the bells, hark to the bells,
This is the day, day of the King!
Peal out the news oer hill and dale,
And 'round the town telling the tale.
Hark to the bells, hark to the bells,
Telling us all Jesus is King!

Come one and all happily sing
Songs of goodwill, o let them sing.

Ring, silv'ry bells, Sing, joyous bells!

Strongly they chime, sound with a rhyme,
Christmas is here, welcome the King!
Hark to the bells, hark to the bells,
Telling us all Jesus is King!

Ring! Ring! Bells.

COVENTRY CAROL

1. Lullay, thou little tiny child
By by, lully, lullay.
Lullay, thou little tiny child,
By by, lully, lullay.

2. O sisters too, how may we do,
For to preserve this day.
This poor youngling for whome we sing.
By by, lully, lullay.

3. Herod the king, in his raging,
Charged he hath this day.
His men of might, in his own sight,
All young children to slay.

4. That woe is me, poor child for thee!
And ever morn and day,
For thy parting neither say nor sing
By by, lully lullay!

THE FIRST NOEL

1. The first noel, the angel did say
Was to certain poor shepherds in fields as they lay;
In fields where they lay keeping their sheep,
On a cold winter's night that was so deep.
Refrain
Noel, noel, noel, noel,
Born is the King of Israel.

2. They looked up and saw a star
Shining in the East, beyond them far;
And to the earth it gave great light,
And so it continued both day and night.
Refrain

3. And by the light of that same star,
Three wise men came for country far;
To seek for a King was their intent,
And to follow the star wherever it went
Refrain

4. This star drew night to the northwest,
O'er Bethlehem it took its rest;
And there it did both stop and stay,
Right over the place where Jesus lay.
Refrain

5. Then entered in those wise men three,
Full reverently upon their knee;
And offered there in His presence,
Their gold, and myrrh, and frankincense.
Refrain

GO TELL IT ON THE MOUNTAIN

1. While shepherds kept their watching
O'er silent flocks by night,
Behold throughout the heavens
There shone a holy light.

Go, tell it on the mountain,
Over the hills and everywhere,
Go, tell it on the mountain
That Jesus Christ is born.

2. The shepherds feared and trembled
When lo! above the earth
Rang out the angel chorus
That hailed our Savior's birth.

Go, tell it on the mountain,
Over the hills and everywhere,
Go, tell it on the mountain
That Jesus Christ is born.

HARK! THE HERALD ANGELS SING

1. Hark! The herald angels sing,
"Glory to the newborn King!
Peace on earth, and mercy mild,
God and sinners reconciled."

Joyful all ye nations rise,
Join the triumph of the skies;
With th'angelic host proclaim,
"Christ is born in Bethlehem."

Hark! The herald angels sing,
"Glory to the newborn King!"

2. Christ, by highest heaven adored,
Christ, the everlasting Lord,
Late in time behold him come,
Offspring of a Virgin's womb.
Veiled in flesh the Godhead see;
Hail, the incarnate Deity,
Pleased as Man with man to dwell,
Jesus, our Immanuel!

Hark! The herald angels sing,
"Glory to the newborn King!"

3. Hail, the heaven-born Prince of Peace!
Hail, the Sun of Righteousness!
Light and life to all he brings,
Risen with healing in his wings.
Mild he lays his glory by,
Born that man no more may die,
Born to raise the sons of earth,
Born to give them second birth.

Hark! The herald angels sing,
"Glory to the newborn King!"

GOOD KING WENCESLAS

1. Good King Wenceslas looked out
On the feast of Stephen
When the snow lay 'round about,
Deep and crisp and even.
Brightly shown the moon that night,
Though the frost was cruel.
When a poor man came in sight,
Gathering winter fuel.

2. "Hither page, and stand by me,
If thou know'st it, telling,
Yonder peasant, who is he?
Where and what his dwelling?"
"Sire, he lives a good league hence,
Underneath the mountain;
Right against the forest fence,
By Saint Agnes' fountain."

3. "Bring me flesh, and bring me wine,
Bring me pine-logs hither;
Thou and I will see him dine
When we bear them thither."
Page and monarch forth they went,
Forth they went together;
Through the rude winds wild lament:
And the bitter weather.

4. "Sire, the night is darker now,
And the wind blows stronger;
Fails my heart, I know not how,
I can go not longer."
"Mark my footsteps, my good page,
Tread thou in them boldly:
Thou shalt find the winter's rage
Freeze thy blood less coldly."

5. In his master's steps he trod,
Where the snow lay dinted;
Heat was in the very sod
Which the saint had printed.
Therefore, Christian men, be sure,
Wealth or rank possessing,
Ye who now will bless the poor,
Shall yourselves find blessing.

IT CAME UPON THE MIDNIGHT CLEAR

1. It came upon the midnight clear,
That glorious song of old,
From angels bending near the earth
To touch their harps of gold.

Peace on the earth, good will to men
From heaven's all gracious King!

The world in solemn stillness lay
To hear the angels sing.

2. Still through the cloven they come,
With peaceful wings unfurled
And still their heavenly music floats
O'er all the weary world;
Above its sad and lowly plains
They bend on hovering wing,
And ever o'er its Babel sounds
The blessed angels sing.

3. Yet with the woes of sin and strife
The world hath suffered long;
Beneath the angel-strain have rolled
Two thousand years of wrong;
And man, at war with man, hears not
The love song which they bring:
O hush the noise, ye men of strife,
And hear the angels sing.

4. And ye, beneath life's crushing load,
Whose forms are bending low,
Who toil along the climbing way
With painful steps and slow:
Look now! for glad and golden hours
Come swiftly on the wing;
O rest beside the weary road,
And hear the angels sing.

5. For lo! the days are hastening on,
By prophet-bards foretold,
When, with the ever-circling years,
Shall come the Age of Gold;
When peace shall over all the earth
Its heavenly splendors fling,
And all the world give back the song
Which now the angels sing.

LYRICS FOR

Singalong Christmas Carols

ANGELS FROM THE REALMS OF GLORY

1. Angels from the realms of glory,
Wing your flight o'er all the earth,
Ye who sang creation's story,
Now proclaim Messiah's birth.

Come and worship! Come and worship!
Worship Christ the newborn King!

2. Sages, leave your contemplations,
Brighter visions beam afar,
Seek the great Desire of nations
Ye have seen His natal star.

Come and worship! Come and worship!
Worship Christ the newborn King!

3. Sages, leave your contemplations,
Brighter visions beam afar;
Seek the great Desire of nations,
Ye have seen his natal star.

Come and worship! Come and worship!
Worship Christ the newborn King!

4. All creation, join in praising
God, the Father, Spirit, Son,
Evermore your voices raising
To the eternal Three in One.

Come and worship! Come and worship!
Worship Christ the newborn King!

ANGELS WE HAVE HEARD ON HIGH

1. Angels we have heard on high
Sweetly singing o'er the plains,
And the mountains in reply
Echoing their joyous strains.

Gloria in excelsis Deo,
Gloria in excelsis Deo.

2. Shepherds, why this jubilee?
Why your joyous strains prolong?
What the gladsome tidings be
Which inspire your heavenly song?

Gloria in excelsis Deo,
Gloria in excelsis Deo.

3. Come to Bethlehem and see
Him whose birth the angels sing;
Come, adore on bended knee
Christ, the Lord, the new-born King.

Gloria in excelsis Deo,
Gloria, in excelsis Deo.

4. See him in a manger laid
Whom the angels praise above;
Mary, Joseph, lend your aid,
While we raise our hearts in love.

Gloria in excelsis Deo,
Gloria in excelsis Deo.

AWAY IN A MANGER

1. Away in a manger, no crib for a bed,
The little Lord Jesus laid down His
sweet head.
The stars in the sky looked down
where He lay,
The little Lord Jesus, asleep on the hay.

2. The cattle are lowing, the baby awakes,
But Little Lord Jesus, no crying
He makes.
I love Thee, Lord Jesus, look down from
the sky,
And stay by my cradle till morning
is nigh.

3. Be near me, Lord Jesus; I ask Thee to stay
Close by me forever, and love me, I pray.
Bless all the dear children in Thy
tender care,
And fit us for heaven, to live with
Thee there.

CAROL OF THE BELLS

Hark to the bells, hark to the bells,
Telling us all Jesus is King!
Strongly they chime, sound with
a rhyme,
Christmas is here! Welcome the King.
Hark to the bells, hark to the bells,
This is the day, day of the King!
Peal out the news oer hill and dale,
And 'round the town telling the tale.
Hark to the bells, hark to the bells,
Telling us all Jesus is King!

Come one and all happily sing
Songs of goodwill, o let them sing.

Ring, silv'ry bells, Sing, joyous bells!

Strongly they chime, sound with a rhyme,
Christmas is here, welcome the King!
Hark to the bells, hark to the bells,
Telling us all Jesus is King!

Ring! Ring! Bells.

COVENTRY CAROL

1. Lullay, thou little tiny child
By by, lully, lullay.
Lullay, thou little tiny child,
By by, lully, lullay.

2. O sisters too, how may we do,
For to preserve this day.
This poor youngling for whome we sing.
By by, lully, lullay.

3. Herod the king, in his raging,
Charged he hath this day.
His men of might, in his own sight,
All young children to slay.

4. That woe is me, poor child for thee!
And ever morn and day,
For thy parting neither say nor sing
By by, lully lullay!

THE FIRST NOEL

1. The first noel, the angel did say
Was to certain poor shepherds in
fields as they lay;
In fields where they lay keeping
their sheep,
On a cold winter's night that was
so deep.
Refrain
Noel, noel, noel, noel,
Born is the King of Israel.

2. They looked up and saw a star
Shining in the East, beyond them far;
And to the earth it gave great light,
And so it continued both day and night.
Refrain

3. And by the light of that same star,
Three wise men came for country far;
To seek for a King was their intent,
And to follow the star wherever it went
Refrain

4. This star drew night to the northwest,
O'er Bethlehem it took its rest;
And there it did both stop and stay,
Right over the place where Jesus lay.
Refrain

5. Then entered in those wise men three,
Full reverently upon their knee;
And offered there in His presence,
Their gold, and myrrh, and
frankincense.
Refrain

GO TELL IT ON THE MOUNTAIN

1. While shepherds kept their watching
O'er silent flocks by night,
Behold throughout the heavens
There shone a holy light.

Go, tell it on the mountain,
Over the hills and everywhere,
Go, tell it on the mountain
That Jesus Christ is born.

2. The shepherds feared and trembled
When lo! above the earth
Rang out the angel chorus
That hailed our Savior's birth.

Go, tell it on the mountain,
Over the hills and everywhere,
Go, tell it on the mountain
That Jesus Christ is born.

HARK! THE HERALD ANGELS SING

1. Hark! The herald angels sing,
"Glory to the newborn King!
Peace on earth, and mercy mild,
God and sinners reconciled."

Joyful all ye nations rise,
Join the triumph of the skies;
With th'angelic host proclaim,
"Christ is born in Bethlehem."

Hark! The herald angels sing,
"Glory to the newborn King!"

2. Christ, by highest heaven adored,
Christ, the everlasting Lord,
Late in time behold him come,
Offspring of a Virgin's womb.
Veiled in flesh the Godhead see;
Hail, the incarnate Deity,
Pleased as Man with man to dwell,
Jesus, our Immanuel!

Hark! The herald angels sing,
"Glory to the newborn King!"

3. Hail, the heaven-born Prince of Peace!
Hail, the Sun of Righteousness!
Light and life to all he brings,
Risen with healing in his wings.
Mild he lays his glory by,
Born that man no more may die,
Born to raise the sons of earth,
Born to give them second birth.

Hark! The herald angels sing,
"Glory to the newborn King!"

GOOD KING WENCESLAS

1. Good King Wenceslas looked out
On the feast of Stephen
When the snow lay 'round about,
Deep and crisp and even.
Brightly shown the moon that night,
Though the frost was cruel.
When a poor man came in sight,
Gathering winter fuel.

2. "Hither page, and stand by me,
If thou know'st it, telling,
Yonder peasant, who is he?
Where and what his dwelling?"
"Sire, he lives a good league hence,
Underneath the mountain;
Right against the forest fence,
By Saint Agnes' fountain."

3. "Bring me flesh, and bring me wine,
Bring me pine-logs hither;
Thou and I will see him dine
When we bear them thither."
Page and monarch forth they went,
Forth they went together;
Through the rude winds wild lament:
And the bitter weather.

4. "Sire, the night is darker now,
And the wind blows stronger;
Fails my heart, I know not how,
I can go not longer."
"Mark my footsteps, my good page,
Tread thou in them boldly:
Thou shalt find the winter's rage
Freeze thy blood less coldly."

5. In his master's steps he trod,
Where the snow lay dinted;
Heat was in the very sod
Which the saint had printed.
Therefore, Christian men, be sure,
Wealth or rank possessing,
Ye who now will bless the poor,
Shall yourselves find blessing.

IT CAME UPON THE MIDNIGHT CLEAR

1. It came upon the midnight clear,
That glorious song of old,
From angels bending near the earth
To touch their harps of gold.

Peace on the earth, good will to men
From heaven's all gracious King!

The world in solemn stillness lay
To hear the angels sing.

2. Still through the cloven they come,
With peaceful wings unfurled
And still their heavenly music floats
O'er all the weary world;
Above its sad and lowly plains
They bend on hovering wing,
And ever o'er its Babel sounds
The blessed angels sing.

3. Yet with the woes of sin and strife
The world hath suffered long;
Beneath the angel-strain have rolled
Two thousand years of wrong;
And man, at war with man, hears not
The love song which they bring:
O hush the noise, ye men of strife,
And hear the angels sing.

4. And ye, beneath life's crushing load,
Whose forms are bending low,
Who toil along the climbing way
With painful steps and slow:
Look now! for glad and golden hours
Come swiftly on the wing;
O rest beside the weary road,
And hear the angels sing.

5. For lo! the days are hastening on,
By prophet-bards foretold,
When, with the ever-circling years,
Shall come the Age of Gold;
When peace shall over all the earth
Its heavenly splendors fling,
And all the world give back the song
Which now the angels sing.

LYRICS FOR

Singalong Christmas Carols

ANGELS FROM THE REALMS OF GLORY

1. Angels from the realms of glory,
Wing your flight o'er all the earth,
Ye who sang creation's story,
Now proclaim Messiah's birth.

Come and worship! Come and worship!
Worship Christ the newborn King!

2. Sages, leave your contemplations,
Brighter visions beam afar,
Seek the great Desire of nations
Ye have seen His natal star.

Come and worship! Come and worship!
Worship Christ the newborn King!

3. Sages, leave your contemplations,
Brighter visions beam afar;
Seek the great Desire of nations,
Ye have seen his natal star.

Come and worship! Come and worship!
Worship Christ the newborn King!

4. All creation, join in praising
God, the Father, Spirit, Son,
Evermore your voices raising
To the eternal Three in One.

Come and worship! Come and worship!
Worship Christ the newborn King!

ANGELS WE HAVE HEARD ON HIGH

1. Angels we have heard on high
Sweetly singing o'er the plains,
And the mountains in reply
Echoing their joyous strains.

Gloria in excelsis Deo,
Gloria in excelsis Deo.

2. Shepherds, why this jubilee?
Why your joyous strains prolong?
What the gladsome tidings be
Which inspire your heavenly song?

Gloria in excelsis Deo,
Gloria in excelsis Deo.

3. Come to Bethlehem and see
Him whose birth the angels sing;
Come, adore on bended knee
Christ, the Lord, the new-born King.

Gloria in excelsis Deo,
Gloria, in excelsis Deo.

4. See him in a manger laid
Whom the angels praise above;
Mary, Joseph, lend your aid,
While we raise our hearts in love.

Gloria in excelsis Deo,
Gloria in excelsis Deo.

AWAY IN A MANGER

1. Away in a manger, no crib for a bed,
The little Lord Jesus laid down His
sweet head.
The stars in the sky looked down
where He lay,
The little Lord Jesus, asleep on the hay.

2. The cattle are lowing, the baby awakes,
But Little Lord Jesus, no crying
He makes.
I love Thee, Lord Jesus, look down from
the sky,
And stay by my cradle till morning
is nigh.

3. Be near me, Lord Jesus; I ask Thee to stay
Close by me forever, and love me, I pray.
Bless all the dear children in Thy
tender care,
And fit us for heaven, to live with
Thee there.

CAROL OF THE BELLS

Hark to the bells, hark to the bells,
Telling us all Jesus is King!
Strongly they chime, sound with
a rhyme,
Christmas is here! Welcome the King.
Hark to the bells, hark to the bells,
This is the day, day of the King!
Peal out the news oer hill and dale,
And 'round the town telling the tale.
Hark to the bells, hark to the bells,
Telling us all Jesus is King!

Come one and all happily sing
Songs of goodwill, o let them sing.

Ring, silv'ry bells, Sing, joyous bells!

Strongly they chime, sound with a rhyme,
Christmas is here, welcome the King!
Hark to the bells, hark to the bells,
Telling us all Jesus is King!

Ring! Ring! Bells.

COVENTRY CAROL

1. Lullay, thou little tiny child
By by, lully, lullay.
Lullay, thou little tiny child,
By by, lully, lullay.

2. O sisters too, how may we do,
For to preserve this day.
This poor youngling for whome we sing.
By by, lully, lullay.

3. Herod the king, in his raging,
Charged he hath this day.
His men of might, in his own sight,
All young children to slay.

4. That woe is me, poor child for thee!
And ever morn and day,
For thy parting neither say nor sing
By by, lully lullay!

THE FIRST NOEL

1. The first noel, the angel did say
Was to certain poor shepherds in
fields as they lay;
In fields where they lay keeping
their sheep,
On a cold winter's night that was
so deep.
Refrain
Noel, noel, noel, noel,
Born is the King of Israel.

2. They looked up and saw a star
Shining in the East, beyond them far;
And to the earth it gave great light,
And so it continued both day and night.
Refrain

3. And by the light of that same star,
Three wise men came for country far;
To seek for a King was their intent,
And to follow the star wherever it went
Refrain

4. This star drew night to the northwest,
O'er Bethlehem it took its rest;
And there it did both stop and stay,
Right over the place where Jesus lay.
Refrain

5. Then entered in those wise men three,
Full reverently upon their knee;
And offered there in His presence,
Their gold, and myrrh, and
frankincense.
Refrain

GO TELL IT ON THE MOUNTAIN

1. While shepherds kept their watching
O'er silent flocks by night,
Behold throughout the heavens
There shone a holy light.

Go, tell it on the mountain,
Over the hills and everywhere,
Go, tell it on the mountain
That Jesus Christ is born.

2. The shepherds feared and trembled
When lo! above the earth
Rang out the angel chorus
That hailed our Savior's birth.

Go, tell it on the mountain,
Over the hills and everywhere,
Go, tell it on the mountain
That Jesus Christ is born.

HARK! THE HERALD ANGELS SING

1. Hark! The herald angels sing,
"Glory to the newborn King!
Peace on earth, and mercy mild,
God and sinners reconciled."

Joyful all ye nations rise,
Join the triumph of the skies;
With th'angelic host proclaim,
"Christ is born in Bethlehem."

Hark! The herald angels sing,
"Glory to the newborn King!"

2. Christ, by highest heaven adored,
Christ, the everlasting Lord,
Late in time behold him come,
Offspring of a Virgin's womb.
Veiled in flesh the Godhead see;
Hail, the incarnate Deity,
Pleased as Man with man to dwell,
Jesus, our Immanuel!

Hark! The herald angels sing,
"Glory to the newborn King!"

3. Hail, the heaven-born Prince of Peace!
Hail, the Sun of Righteousness!
Light and life to all he brings,
Risen with healing in his wings.
Mild he lays his glory by,
Born that man no more may die,
Born to raise the sons of earth,
Born to give them second birth.

Hark! The herald angels sing,
"Glory to the newborn King!"

GOOD KING WENCESLAS

1. Good King Wenceslas looked out
On the feast of Stephen
When the snow lay 'round about,
Deep and crisp and even.
Brightly shown the moon that night,
Though the frost was cruel.
When a poor man came in sight,
Gathering winter fuel.

2. "Hither page, and stand by me,
If thou know'st it, telling,
Yonder peasant, who is he?
Where and what his dwelling?"
"Sire, he lives a good league hence,
Underneath the mountain;
Right against the forest fence,
By Saint Agnes' fountain."

3. "Bring me flesh, and bring me wine,
Bring me pine-logs hither;
Thou and I will see him dine
When we bear them thither."
Page and monarch forth they went,
Forth they went together;
Through the rude winds wild lament:
And the bitter weather.

4. "Sire, the night is darker now,
And the wind blows stronger;
Fails my heart, I know not how,
I can go not longer."
"Mark my footsteps, my good page,
Tread thou in them boldly:
Thou shalt find the winter's rage
Freeze thy blood less coldly."

5. In his master's steps he trod,
Where the snow lay dinted;
Heat was in the very sod
Which the saint had printed.
Therefore, Christian men, be sure,
Wealth or rank possessing,
Ye who now will bless the poor,
Shall yourselves find blessing.

IT CAME UPON THE MIDNIGHT CLEAR

1. It came upon the midnight clear,
That glorious song of old,
From angels bending near the earth
To touch their harps of gold.

Peace on the earth, good will to men
From heaven's all gracious King!

The world in solemn stillness lay
To hear the angels sing.

2. Still through the cloven they come,
With peaceful wings unfurled
And still their heavenly music floats
O'er all the weary world;
Above its sad and lowly plains
They bend on hovering wing,
And ever o'er its Babel sounds
The blessed angels sing.

3. Yet with the woes of sin and strife
The world hath suffered long;
Beneath the angel-strain have rolled
Two thousand years of wrong;
And man, at war with man, hears not
The love song which they bring:
O hush the noise, ye men of strife,
And hear the angels sing.

4. And ye, beneath life's crushing load,
Whose forms are bending low,
Who toil along the climbing way
With painful steps and slow:
Look now! for glad and golden hours
Come swiftly on the wing;
O rest beside the weary road,
And hear the angels sing.

5. For lo! the days are hastening on,
By prophet-bards foretold,
When, with the ever-circling years,
Shall come the Age of Gold;
When peace shall over all the earth
Its heavenly splendors fling,
And all the world give back the song
Which now the angels sing.

LYRICS FOR

Singalong Christmas Carols

ANGELS FROM THE REALMS OF GLORY

1. Angels from the realms of glory,
Wing your flight o'er all the earth,
Ye who sang creation's story,
Now proclaim Messiah's birth.

Come and worship! Come and worship!
Worship Christ the newborn King!

2. Sages, leave your contemplations,
Brighter visions beam afar,
Seek the great Desire of nations
Ye have seen His natal star.

Come and worship! Come and worship!
Worship Christ the newborn King!

3. Sages, leave your contemplations,
Brighter visions beam afar;
Seek the great Desire of nations,
Ye have seen his natal star.

Come and worship! Come and worship!
Worship Christ the newborn King!

4. All creation, join in praising
God, the Father, Spirit, Son,
Evermore your voices raising
To the eternal Three in One.

Come and worship! Come and worship!
Worship Christ the newborn King!

ANGELS WE HAVE HEARD ON HIGH

1. Angels we have heard on high
Sweetly singing o'er the plains,
And the mountains in reply
Echoing their joyous strains.

Gloria in excelsis Deo,
Gloria in excelsis Deo.

2. Shepherds, why this jubilee?
Why your joyous strains prolong?
What the gladsome tidings be
Which inspire your heavenly song?

Gloria in excelsis Deo,
Gloria in excelsis Deo.

3. Come to Bethlehem and see
Him whose birth the angels sing;
Come, adore on bended knee
Christ, the Lord, the new-born King.

Gloria in excelsis Deo,
Gloria, in excelsis Deo.

4. See him in a manger laid
Whom the angels praise above;
Mary, Joseph, lend your aid,
While we raise our hearts in love.

Gloria in excelsis Deo,
Gloria in excelsis Deo.

AWAY IN A MANGER

1. Away in a manger, no crib for a bed,
The little Lord Jesus laid down His sweet head.
The stars in the sky looked down where He lay,
The little Lord Jesus, asleep on the hay.

2. The cattle are lowing, the baby awakes,
But Little Lord Jesus, no crying He makes.
I love Thee, Lord Jesus, look down from the sky,
And stay by my cradle till morning is nigh.

3. Be near me, Lord Jesus; I ask Thee to stay
Close by me forever, and love me, I pray.
Bless all the dear children in Thy tender care,
And fit us for heaven, to live with Thee there.

CAROL OF THE BELLS

Hark to the bells, hark to the bells,
Telling us all Jesus is King!
Strongly they chime, sound with a rhyme,
Christmas is here! Welcome the King.
Hark to the bells, hark to the bells,
This is the day, day of the King!
Peal out the news oer hill and dale,
And 'round the town telling the tale.
Hark to the bells, hark to the bells,
Telling us all Jesus is King!

Come one and all happily sing
Songs of goodwill, o let them sing.

Ring, silv'ry bells, Sing, joyous bells!

Strongly they chime, sound with a rhyme,
Christmas is here, welcome the King!
Hark to the bells, hark to the bells,
Telling us all Jesus is King!

Ring! Ring! Bells.

COVENTRY CAROL

1. Lullay, thou little tiny child
By by, lully, lullay.
Lullay, thou little tiny child,
By by, lully, lullay.

2. O sisters too, how may we do,
For to preserve this day.
This poor youngling for whome we sing.
By by, lully, lullay.

3. Herod the king, in his raging,
Charged he hath this day.
His men of might, in his own sight,
All young children to slay.

4. That woe is me, poor child for thee!
And ever morn and day,
For thy parting neither say nor sing
By by, lully lullay!

THE FIRST NOEL

1. The first noel, the angel did say
Was to certain poor shepherds in fields as they lay;
In fields where they lay keeping their sheep,
On a cold winter's night that was so deep.
Refrain
Noel, noel, noel, noel,
Born is the King of Israel.

2. They looked up and saw a star
Shining in the East, beyond them far;
And to the earth it gave great light,
And so it continued both day and night.
Refrain

3. And by the light of that same star,
Three wise men came for country far;
To seek for a King was their intent,
And to follow the star wherever it went
Refrain

4. This star drew night to the northwest,
O'er Bethlehem it took its rest;
And there it did both stop and stay,
Right over the place where Jesus lay.
Refrain

5. Then entered in those wise men three,
Full reverently upon their knee;
And offered there in His presence,
Their gold, and myrrh, and frankincense.
Refrain

GO TELL IT ON THE MOUNTAIN

1. While shepherds kept their watching
   O'er silent flocks by night,
   Behold throughout the heavens
   There shone a holy light.

   Go, tell it on the mountain,
   Over the hills and everywhere,
   Go, tell it on the mountain
   That Jesus Christ is born.

2. The shepherds feared and trembled
   When lo! above the earth
   Rang out the angel chorus
   That hailed our Savior's birth.

   Go, tell it on the mountain,
   Over the hills and everywhere,
   Go, tell it on the mountain
   That Jesus Christ is born.

HARK! THE HERALD ANGELS SING

1. Hark! The herald angels sing,
   "Glory to the newborn King!
   Peace on earth, and mercy mild,
   God and sinners reconciled."

   Joyful all ye nations rise,
   Join the triumph of the skies;
   With th'angelic host proclaim,
   "Christ is born in Bethlehem."

   Hark! The herald angels sing,
   "Glory to the newborn King!"

2. Christ, by highest heaven adored,
   Christ, the everlasting Lord,
   Late in time behold him come,
   Offspring of a Virgin's womb.
   Veiled in flesh the Godhead see;
   Hail, the incarnate Deity,
   Pleased as Man with man to dwell,
   Jesus, our Immanuel!

   Hark! The herald angels sing,
   "Glory to the newborn King!"

3. Hail, the heaven-born Prince of Peace!
   Hail, the Sun of Righteousness!
   Light and life to all he brings,
   Risen with healing in his wings.
   Mild he lays his glory by,
   Born that man no more may die,
   Born to raise the sons of earth,
   Born to give them second birth.

   Hark! The herald angels sing,
   "Glory to the newborn King!"

GOOD KING WENCESLAS

1. Good King Wenceslas looked out
   On the feast of Stephen
   When the snow lay 'round about,
   Deep and crisp and even.
   Brightly shown the moon that night,
   Though the frost was cruel.
   When a poor man came in sight,
   Gathering winter fuel.

2. "Hither page, and stand by me,
   If thou know'st it, telling,
   Yonder peasant, who is he?
   Where and what his dwelling?"
   "Sire, he lives a good league hence,
   Underneath the mountain;
   Right against the forest fence,
   By Saint Agnes' fountain."

3. "Bring me flesh, and bring me wine,
   Bring me pine-logs hither;
   Thou and I will see him dine
   When we bear them thither."
   Page and monarch forth they went,
   Forth they went together;
   Through the rude winds wild lament:
   And the bitter weather.

4. "Sire, the night is darker now,
   And the wind blows stronger;
   Fails my heart, I know not how,
   I can go not longer."
   "Mark my footsteps, my good page,
   Tread thou in them boldly:
   Thou shalt find the winter's rage
   Freeze thy blood less coldly."

5. In his master's steps he trod,
   Where the snow lay dinted;
   Heat was in the very sod
   Which the saint had printed.
   Therefore, Christian men, be sure,
   Wealth or rank possessing,
   Ye who now will bless the poor,
   Shall yourselves find blessing.

IT CAME UPON THE MIDNIGHT CLEAR

1. It came upon the midnight clear,
   That glorious song of old,
   From angels bending near the earth
   To touch their harps of gold.

   Peace on the earth, good will to men
   From heaven's all gracious King!

   The world in solemn stillness lay
   To hear the angels sing.

2. Still through the cloven they come,
   With peaceful wings unfurled
   And still their heavenly music floats
   O'er all the weary world;
   Above its sad and lowly plains
   They bend on hovering wing,
   And ever o'er its Babel sounds
   The blessed angels sing.

3. Yet with the woes of sin and strife
   The world hath suffered long;
   Beneath the angel-strain have rolled
   Two thousand years of wrong;
   And man, at war with man, hears not
   The love song which they bring:
   O hush the noise, ye men of strife,
   And hear the angels sing.

4. And ye, beneath life's crushing load,
   Whose forms are bending low,
   Who toil along the climbing way
   With painful steps and slow:
   Look now! for glad and golden hours
   Come swiftly on the wing;
   O rest beside the weary road,
   And hear the angels sing.

5. For lo! the days are hastening on,
   By prophet-bards foretold,
   When, with the ever-circling years,
   Shall come the Age of Gold;
   When peace shall over all the earth
   Its heavenly splendors fling,
   And all the world give back the song
   Which now the angels sing.

LYRICS FOR

Singalong Christmas Carols

ANGELS FROM THE REALMS OF GLORY

1. Angels from the realms of glory,
Wing your flight o'er all the earth,
Ye who sang creation's story,
Now proclaim Messiah's birth.

Come and worship! Come and worship!
Worship Christ the newborn King!

2. Sages, leave your contemplations,
Brighter visions beam afar,
Seek the great Desire of nations
Ye have seen His natal star.

Come and worship! Come and worship!
Worship Christ the newborn King!

3. Sages, leave your contemplations,
Brighter visions beam afar;
Seek the great Desire of nations,
Ye have seen his natal star.

Come and worship! Come and worship!
Worship Christ the newborn King!

4. All creation, join in praising
God, the Father, Spirit, Son,
Evermore your voices raising
To the eternal Three in One.

Come and worship! Come and worship!
Worship Christ the newborn King!

ANGELS WE HAVE HEARD ON HIGH

1. Angels we have heard on high
Sweetly singing o'er the plains,
And the mountains in reply
Echoing their joyous strains.

Gloria in excelsis Deo,
Gloria in excelsis Deo.

2. Shepherds, why this jubilee?
Why your joyous strains prolong?
What the gladsome tidings be
Which inspire your heavenly song?

Gloria in excelsis Deo,
Gloria in excelsis Deo.

3. Come to Bethlehem and see
Him whose birth the angels sing;
Come, adore on bended knee
Christ, the Lord, the new-born King.

Gloria in excelsis Deo,
Gloria, in excelsis Deo.

4. See him in a manger laid
Whom the angels praise above;
Mary, Joseph, lend your aid,
While we raise our hearts in love.

Gloria in excelsis Deo,
Gloria in excelsis Deo.

AWAY IN A MANGER

1. Away in a manger, no crib for a bed,
The little Lord Jesus laid down His
sweet head.
The stars in the sky looked down
where He lay,
The little Lord Jesus, asleep on the hay.

2. The cattle are lowing, the baby awakes,
But Little Lord Jesus, no crying
He makes.
I love Thee, Lord Jesus, look down from
the sky,
And stay by my cradle till morning
is nigh.

3. Be near me, Lord Jesus; I ask Thee to stay
Close by me forever, and love me, I pray.
Bless all the dear children in Thy
tender care,
And fit us for heaven, to live with
Thee there.

CAROL OF THE BELLS

Hark to the bells, hark to the bells,
Telling us all Jesus is King!
Strongly they chime, sound with
a rhyme,
Christmas is here! Welcome the King.
Hark to the bells, hark to the bells,
This is the day, day of the King!
Peal out the news oer hill and dale,
And 'round the town telling the tale.
Hark to the bells, hark to the bells,
Telling us all Jesus is King!

Come one and all happily sing
Songs of goodwill, o let them sing.

Ring, silv'ry bells, Sing, joyous bells!

Strongly they chime, sound with a rhyme,
Christmas is here, welcome the King!
Hark to the bells, hark to the bells,
Telling us all Jesus is King!

Ring! Ring! Bells.

COVENTRY CAROL

1. Lullay, thou little tiny child
By by, lully, lullay.
Lullay, thou little tiny child,
By by, lully, lullay.

2. O sisters too, how may we do,
For to preserve this day.
This poor youngling for whome we sing.
By by, lully, lullay.

3. Herod the king, in his raging,
Charged he hath this day.
His men of might, in his own sight,
All young children to slay.

4. That woe is me, poor child for thee!
And ever morn and day,
For thy parting neither say nor sing
By by, lully lullay!

THE FIRST NOEL

1. The first noel, the angel did say
Was to certain poor shepherds in
fields as they lay;
In fields where they lay keeping
their sheep,
On a cold winter's night that was
so deep.
Refrain
Noel, noel, noel, noel,
Born is the King of Israel.

2. They looked up and saw a star
Shining in the East, beyond them far;
And to the earth it gave great light,
And so it continued both day and night.
Refrain

3. And by the light of that same star,
Three wise men came for country far;
To seek for a King was their intent,
And to follow the star wherever it went
Refrain

4. This star drew night to the northwest,
O'er Bethlehem it took its rest;
And there it did both stop and stay,
Right over the place where Jesus lay.
Refrain

5. Then entered in those wise men three,
Full reverently upon their knee;
And offered there in His presence,
Their gold, and myrrh, and
frankincense.
Refrain

GO TELL IT ON THE MOUNTAIN

1. While shepherds kept their watching
O'er silent flocks by night,
Behold throughout the heavens
There shone a holy light.

Go, tell it on the mountain,
Over the hills and everywhere,
Go, tell it on the mountain
That Jesus Christ is born.

2. The shepherds feared and trembled
When lo! above the earth
Rang out the angel chorus
That hailed our Savior's birth.

Go, tell it on the mountain,
Over the hills and everywhere,
Go, tell it on the mountain
That Jesus Christ is born.

HARK! THE HERALD ANGELS SING

1. Hark! The herald angels sing,
"Glory to the newborn King!
Peace on earth, and mercy mild,
God and sinners reconciled."

Joyful all ye nations rise,
Join the triumph of the skies;
With th'angelic host proclaim,
"Christ is born in Bethlehem."

Hark! The herald angels sing,
"Glory to the newborn King!"

2. Christ, by highest heaven adored,
Christ, the everlasting Lord,
Late in time behold him come,
Offspring of a Virgin's womb.
Veiled in flesh the Godhead see;
Hail, the incarnate Deity,
Pleased as Man with man to dwell,
Jesus, our Immanuel!

Hark! The herald angels sing,
"Glory to the newborn King!"

3. Hail, the heaven-born Prince of Peace!
Hail, the Sun of Righteousness!
Light and life to all he brings,
Risen with healing in his wings.
Mild he lays his glory by,
Born that man no more may die,
Born to raise the sons of earth,
Born to give them second birth.

Hark! The herald angels sing,
"Glory to the newborn King!"

GOOD KING WENCESLAS

1. Good King Wenceslas looked out
On the feast of Stephen
When the snow lay 'round about,
Deep and crisp and even.
Brightly shown the moon that night,
Though the frost was cruel.
When a poor man came in sight,
Gathering winter fuel.

2. "Hither page, and stand by me,
If thou know'st it, telling,
Yonder peasant, who is he?
Where and what his dwelling?"
"Sire, he lives a good league hence,
Underneath the mountain;
Right against the forest fence,
By Saint Agnes' fountain."

3. "Bring me flesh, and bring me wine,
Bring me pine-logs hither;
Thou and I will see him dine
When we bear them thither."
Page and monarch forth they went,
Forth they went together;
Through the rude winds wild lament:
And the bitter weather.

4. "Sire, the night is darker now,
And the wind blows stronger;
Fails my heart, I know not how,
I can go not longer."
"Mark my footsteps, my good page,
Tread thou in them boldly:
Thou shalt find the winter's rage
Freeze thy blood less coldly."

5. In his master's steps he trod,
Where the snow lay dinted;
Heat was in the very sod
Which the saint had printed.
Therefore, Christian men, be sure,
Wealth or rank possessing,
Ye who now will bless the poor,
Shall yourselves find blessing.

IT CAME UPON THE MIDNIGHT CLEAR

1. It came upon the midnight clear,
That glorious song of old,
From angels bending near the earth
To touch their harps of gold.

Peace on the earth, good will to men
From heaven's all gracious King!

The world in solemn stillness lay
To hear the angels sing.

2. Still through the cloven they come,
With peaceful wings unfurled
And still their heavenly music floats
O'er all the weary world;
Above its sad and lowly plains
They bend on hovering wing,
And ever o'er its Babel sounds
The blessed angels sing.

3. Yet with the woes of sin and strife
The world hath suffered long;
Beneath the angel-strain have rolled
Two thousand years of wrong;
And man, at war with man, hears not
The love song which they bring:
O hush the noise, ye men of strife,
And hear the angels sing.

4. And ye, beneath life's crushing load,
Whose forms are bending low,
Who toil along the climbing way
With painful steps and slow:
Look now! for glad and golden hours
Come swiftly on the wing;
O rest beside the weary road,
And hear the angels sing.

5. For lo! the days are hastening on,
By prophet-bards foretold,
When, with the ever-circling years,
Shall come the Age of Gold;
When peace shall over all the earth
Its heavenly splendors fling,
And all the world give back the song
Which now the angels sing.

LYRICS FOR

Singalong Christmas Carols

ANGELS FROM THE REALMS OF GLORY

1. Angels from the realms of glory,
Wing your flight o'er all the earth,
Ye who sang creation's story,
Now proclaim Messiah's birth.

Come and worship! Come and worship!
Worship Christ the newborn King!

2. Sages, leave your contemplations,
Brighter visions beam afar,
Seek the great Desire of nations
Ye have seen His natal star.

Come and worship! Come and worship!
Worship Christ the newborn King!

3. Sages, leave your contemplations,
Brighter visions beam afar;
Seek the great Desire of nations,
Ye have seen his natal star.

Come and worship! Come and worship!
Worship Christ the newborn King!

4. All creation, join in praising
God, the Father, Spirit, Son,
Evermore your voices raising
To the eternal Three in One.

Come and worship! Come and worship!
Worship Christ the newborn King!

ANGELS WE HAVE HEARD ON HIGH

1. Angels we have heard on high
Sweetly singing o'er the plains,
And the mountains in reply
Echoing their joyous strains.

Gloria in excelsis Deo,
Gloria in excelsis Deo.

2. Shepherds, why this jubilee?
Why your joyous strains prolong?
What the gladsome tidings be
Which inspire your heavenly song?

Gloria in excelsis Deo,
Gloria in excelsis Deo.

3. Come to Bethlehem and see
Him whose birth the angels sing;
Come, adore on bended knee
Christ, the Lord, the new-born King.

Gloria in excelsis Deo,
Gloria, in excelsis Deo.

4. See him in a manger laid
Whom the angels praise above;
Mary, Joseph, lend your aid,
While we raise our hearts in love.

Gloria in excelsis Deo,
Gloria in excelsis Deo.

AWAY IN A MANGER

1. Away in a manger, no crib for a bed,
The little Lord Jesus laid down His
sweet head.
The stars in the sky looked down
where He lay,
The little Lord Jesus, asleep on the hay.

2. The cattle are lowing, the baby awakes,
But Little Lord Jesus, no crying
He makes.
I love Thee, Lord Jesus, look down from
the sky,
And stay by my cradle till morning
is nigh.

3. Be near me, Lord Jesus; I ask Thee to stay
Close by me forever, and love me, I pray.
Bless all the dear children in Thy
tender care,
And fit us for heaven, to live with
Thee there.

CAROL OF THE BELLS

Hark to the bells, hark to the bells,
Telling us all Jesus is King!
Strongly they chime, sound with
a rhyme,
Christmas is here! Welcome the King.
Hark to the bells, hark to the bells,
This is the day, day of the King!
Peal out the news oer hill and dale,
And 'round the town telling the tale.
Hark to the bells, hark to the bells,
Telling us all Jesus is King!

Come one and all happily sing
Songs of goodwill, o let them sing.

Ring, silv'ry bells, Sing, joyous bells!

Strongly they chime, sound with a rhyme,
Christmas is here, welcome the King!
Hark to the bells, hark to the bells,
Telling us all Jesus is King!

Ring! Ring! Bells.

COVENTRY CAROL

1. Lullay, thou little tiny child
By by, lully, lullay.
Lullay, thou little tiny child,
By by, lully, lullay.

2. O sisters too, how may we do,
For to preserve this day.
This poor youngling for whome we sing.
By by, lully, lullay.

3. Herod the king, in his raging,
Charged he hath this day.
His men of might, in his own sight,
All young children to slay.

4. That woe is me, poor child for thee!
And ever morn and day,
For thy parting neither say nor sing
By by, lully lullay!

THE FIRST NOEL

1. The first noel, the angel did say
Was to certain poor shepherds in
fields as they lay;
In fields where they lay keeping
their sheep,
On a cold winter's night that was
so deep.
Refrain
Noel, noel, noel, noel,
Born is the King of Israel.

2. They looked up and saw a star
Shining in the East, beyond them far;
And to the earth it gave great light,
And so it continued both day and night.
Refrain

3. And by the light of that same star,
Three wise men came for country far;
To seek for a King was their intent,
And to follow the star wherever it went
Refrain

4. This star drew night to the northwest,
O'er Bethlehem it took its rest;
And there it did both stop and stay,
Right over the place where Jesus lay.
Refrain

5. Then entered in those wise men three,
Full reverently upon their knee;
And offered there in His presence,
Their gold, and myrrh, and
frankincense.
Refrain

GO TELL IT ON THE MOUNTAIN

1. While shepherds kept their watching
O'er silent flocks by night,
Behold throughout the heavens
There shone a holy light.

Go, tell it on the mountain,
Over the hills and everywhere,
Go, tell it on the mountain
That Jesus Christ is born.

2. The shepherds feared and trembled
When lo! above the earth
Rang out the angel chorus
That hailed our Savior's birth.

Go, tell it on the mountain,
Over the hills and everywhere,
Go, tell it on the mountain
That Jesus Christ is born.

HARK! THE HERALD ANGELS SING

1. Hark! The herald angels sing,
"Glory to the newborn King!
Peace on earth, and mercy mild,
God and sinners reconciled."

Joyful all ye nations rise,
Join the triumph of the skies;
With th'angelic host proclaim,
"Christ is born in Bethlehem."

Hark! The herald angels sing,
"Glory to the newborn King!"

2. Christ, by highest heaven adored,
Christ, the everlasting Lord,
Late in time behold him come,
Offspring of a Virgin's womb.
Veiled in flesh the Godhead see;
Hail, the incarnate Deity,
Pleased as Man with man to dwell,
Jesus, our Immanuel!

Hark! The herald angels sing,
"Glory to the newborn King!"

3. Hail, the heaven-born Prince of Peace!
Hail, the Sun of Righteousness!
Light and life to all he brings,
Risen with healing in his wings.
Mild he lays his glory by,
Born that man no more may die,
Born to raise the sons of earth,
Born to give them second birth.

Hark! The herald angels sing,
"Glory to the newborn King!"

GOOD KING WENCESLAS

1. Good King Wenceslas looked out
On the feast of Stephen
When the snow lay 'round about,
Deep and crisp and even.
Brightly shown the moon that night,
Though the frost was cruel.
When a poor man came in sight,
Gathering winter fuel.

2. "Hither page, and stand by me,
If thou know'st it, telling,
Yonder peasant, who is he?
Where and what his dwelling?"
"Sire, he lives a good league hence,
Underneath the mountain;
Right against the forest fence,
By Saint Agnes' fountain."

3. "Bring me flesh, and bring me wine,
Bring me pine-logs hither;
Thou and I will see him dine
When we bear them thither."
Page and monarch forth they went,
Forth they went together;
Through the rude winds wild lament:
And the bitter weather.

4. "Sire, the night is darker now,
And the wind blows stronger;
Fails my heart, I know not how,
I can go not longer."
"Mark my footsteps, my good page,
Tread thou in them boldly:
Thou shalt find the winter's rage
Freeze thy blood less coldly."

5. In his master's steps he trod,
Where the snow lay dinted;
Heat was in the very sod
Which the saint had printed.
Therefore, Christian men, be sure,
Wealth or rank possessing,
Ye who now will bless the poor,
Shall yourselves find blessing.

IT CAME UPON THE MIDNIGHT CLEAR

1. It came upon the midnight clear,
That glorious song of old,
From angels bending near the earth
To touch their harps of gold.

Peace on the earth, good will to men
From heaven's all gracious King!

The world in solemn stillness lay
To hear the angels sing.

2. Still through the cloven they come,
With peaceful wings unfurled
And still their heavenly music floats
O'er all the weary world;
Above its sad and lowly plains
They bend on hovering wing,
And ever o'er its Babel sounds
The blessed angels sing.

3. Yet with the woes of sin and strife
The world hath suffered long;
Beneath the angel-strain have rolled
Two thousand years of wrong;
And man, at war with man, hears not
The love song which they bring:
O hush the noise, ye men of strife,
And hear the angels sing.

4. And ye, beneath life's crushing load,
Whose forms are bending low,
Who toil along the climbing way
With painful steps and slow:
Look now! for glad and golden hours
Come swiftly on the wing;
O rest beside the weary road,
And hear the angels sing.

5. For lo! the days are hastening on,
By prophet-bards foretold,
When, with the ever-circling years,
Shall come the Age of Gold;
When peace shall over all the earth
Its heavenly splendors fling,
And all the world give back the song
Which now the angels sing.

LYRICS FOR

Singalong Christmas Carols

ANGELS FROM THE REALMS OF GLORY

1. Angels from the realms of glory,
Wing your flight o'er all the earth,
Ye who sang creation's story,
Now proclaim Messiah's birth.

Come and worship! Come and worship!
Worship Christ the newborn King!

2. Sages, leave your contemplations,
Brighter visions beam afar,
Seek the great Desire of nations
Ye have seen His natal star.

Come and worship! Come and worship!
Worship Christ the newborn King!

3. Sages, leave your contemplations,
Brighter visions beam afar;
Seek the great Desire of nations,
Ye have seen his natal star.

Come and worship! Come and worship!
Worship Christ the newborn King!

4. All creation, join in praising
God, the Father, Spirit, Son,
Evermore your voices raising
To the eternal Three in One.

Come and worship! Come and worship!
Worship Christ the newborn King!

ANGELS WE HAVE HEARD ON HIGH

1. Angels we have heard on high
Sweetly singing o'er the plains,
And the mountains in reply
Echoing their joyous strains.

Gloria in excelsis Deo,
Gloria in excelsis Deo.

2. Shepherds, why this jubilee?
Why your joyous strains prolong?
What the gladsome tidings be
Which inspire your heavenly song?

Gloria in excelsis Deo,
Gloria in excelsis Deo.

3. Come to Bethlehem and see
Him whose birth the angels sing;
Come, adore on bended knee
Christ, the Lord, the new-born King.

Gloria in excelsis Deo,
Gloria, in excelsis Deo.

4. See him in a manger laid
Whom the angels praise above;
Mary, Joseph, lend your aid,
While we raise our hearts in love.

Gloria in excelsis Deo,
Gloria in excelsis Deo.

AWAY IN A MANGER

1. Away in a manger, no crib for a bed,
The little Lord Jesus laid down His
sweet head.
The stars in the sky looked down
where He lay,
The little Lord Jesus, asleep on the hay.

2. The cattle are lowing, the baby awakes,
But Little Lord Jesus, no crying
He makes.
I love Thee, Lord Jesus, look down from
the sky,
And stay by my cradle till morning
is nigh.

3. Be near me, Lord Jesus; I ask Thee to stay
Close by me forever, and love me, I pray.
Bless all the dear children in Thy
tender care,
And fit us for heaven, to live with
Thee there.

CAROL OF THE BELLS

Hark to the bells, hark to the bells,
Telling us all Jesus is King!
Strongly they chime, sound with
a rhyme,
Christmas is here! Welcome the King.
Hark to the bells, hark to the bells,
This is the day, day of the King!
Peal out the news oer hill and dale,
And 'round the town telling the tale.
Hark to the bells, hark to the bells,
Telling us all Jesus is King!

Come one and all happily sing
Songs of goodwill, o let them sing.

Ring, silv'ry bells, Sing, joyous bells!

Strongly they chime, sound with a rhyme,
Christmas is here, welcome the King!
Hark to the bells, hark to the bells,
Telling us all Jesus is King!

Ring! Ring! Bells.

COVENTRY CAROL

1. Lullay, thou little tiny child
By by, lully, lullay.
Lullay, thou little tiny child,
By by, lully, lullay.

2. O sisters too, how may we do,
For to preserve this day.
This poor youngling for whome we sing.
By by, lully, lullay.

3. Herod the king, in his raging,
Charged he hath this day.
His men of might, in his own sight,
All young children to slay.

4. That woe is me, poor child for thee!
And ever morn and day,
For thy parting neither say nor sing
By by, lully lullay!

THE FIRST NOEL

1. The first noel, the angel did say
Was to certain poor shepherds in
fields as they lay;
In fields where they lay keeping
their sheep,
On a cold winter's night that was
so deep.
Refrain
Noel, noel, noel, noel,
Born is the King of Israel.

2. They looked up and saw a star
Shining in the East, beyond them far;
And to the earth it gave great light,
And so it continued both day and night.
Refrain

3. And by the light of that same star,
Three wise men came for country far;
To seek for a King was their intent,
And to follow the star wherever it went
Refrain

4. This star drew night to the northwest,
O'er Bethlehem it took its rest;
And there it did both stop and stay,
Right over the place where Jesus lay.
Refrain

5. Then entered in those wise men three,
Full reverently upon their knee;
And offered there in His presence,
Their gold, and myrrh, and
frankincense.
Refrain

GO TELL IT ON THE MOUNTAIN

1. While shepherds kept their watching
O'er silent flocks by night,
Behold throughout the heavens
There shone a holy light.

Go, tell it on the mountain,
Over the hills and everywhere,
Go, tell it on the mountain
That Jesus Christ is born.

2. The shepherds feared and trembled
When lo! above the earth
Rang out the angel chorus
That hailed our Savior's birth.

Go, tell it on the mountain,
Over the hills and everywhere,
Go, tell it on the mountain
That Jesus Christ is born.

HARK! THE HERALD ANGELS SING

1. Hark! The herald angels sing,
"Glory to the newborn King!
Peace on earth, and mercy mild,
God and sinners reconciled."

Joyful all ye nations rise,
Join the triumph of the skies;
With th'angelic host proclaim,
"Christ is born in Bethlehem."

Hark! The herald angels sing,
"Glory to the newborn King!"

2. Christ, by highest heaven adored,
Christ, the everlasting Lord,
Late in time behold him come,
Offspring of a Virgin's womb.
Veiled in flesh the Godhead see;
Hail, the incarnate Deity,
Pleased as Man with man to dwell,
Jesus, our Immanuel!

Hark! The herald angels sing,
"Glory to the newborn King!"

3. Hail, the heaven-born Prince of Peace!
Hail, the Sun of Righteousness!
Light and life to all he brings,
Risen with healing in his wings.
Mild he lays his glory by,
Born that man no more may die,
Born to raise the sons of earth,
Born to give them second birth.

Hark! The herald angels sing,
"Glory to the newborn King!"

GOOD KING WENCESLAS

1. Good King Wenceslas looked out
On the feast of Stephen
When the snow lay 'round about,
Deep and crisp and even.
Brightly shown the moon that night,
Though the frost was cruel.
When a poor man came in sight,
Gathering winter fuel.

2. "Hither page, and stand by me,
If thou know'st it, telling,
Yonder peasant, who is he?
Where and what his dwelling?"
"Sire, he lives a good league hence,
Underneath the mountain;
Right against the forest fence,
By Saint Agnes' fountain."

3. "Bring me flesh, and bring me wine,
Bring me pine-logs hither;
Thou and I will see him dine
When we bear them thither."
Page and monarch forth they went,
Forth they went together;
Through the rude winds wild lament:
And the bitter weather.

4. "Sire, the night is darker now,
And the wind blows stronger;
Fails my heart, I know not how,
I can go not longer."
"Mark my footsteps, my good page,
Tread thou in them boldly:
Thou shalt find the winter's rage
Freeze thy blood less coldly."

5. In his master's steps he trod,
Where the snow lay dinted;
Heat was in the very sod
Which the saint had printed.
Therefore, Christian men, be sure,
Wealth or rank possessing,
Ye who now will bless the poor,
Shall yourselves find blessing.

IT CAME UPON THE MIDNIGHT CLEAR

1. It came upon the midnight clear,
That glorious song of old,
From angels bending near the earth
To touch their harps of gold.

Peace on the earth, good will to men
From heaven's all gracious King!

The world in solemn stillness lay
To hear the angels sing.

2. Still through the cloven they come,
With peaceful wings unfurled
And still their heavenly music floats
O'er all the weary world;
Above its sad and lowly plains
They bend on hovering wing,
And ever o'er its Babel sounds
The blessed angels sing.

3. Yet with the woes of sin and strife
The world hath suffered long;
Beneath the angel-strain have rolled
Two thousand years of wrong;
And man, at war with man, hears not
The love song which they bring:
O hush the noise, ye men of strife,
And hear the angels sing.

4. And ye, beneath life's crushing load,
Whose forms are bending low,
Who toil along the climbing way
With painful steps and slow:
Look now! for glad and golden hours
Come swiftly on the wing;
O rest beside the weary road,
And hear the angels sing.

5. For lo! the days are hastening on,
By prophet-bards foretold,
When, with the ever-circling years,
Shall come the Age of Gold;
When peace shall over all the earth
Its heavenly splendors fling,
And all the world give back the song
Which now the angels sing.

LYRICS FOR

Singalong Christmas Carols

ANGELS FROM THE REALMS OF GLORY

1. Angels from the realms of glory,
Wing your flight o'er all the earth,
Ye who sang creation's story,
Now proclaim Messiah's birth.

Come and worship! Come and worship!
Worship Christ the newborn King!

2. Sages, leave your contemplations,
Brighter visions beam afar,
Seek the great Desire of nations
Ye have seen His natal star.

Come and worship! Come and worship!
Worship Christ the newborn King!

3. Sages, leave your contemplations,
Brighter visions beam afar;
Seek the great Desire of nations,
Ye have seen his natal star.

Come and worship! Come and worship!
Worship Christ the newborn King!

4. All creation, join in praising
God, the Father, Spirit, Son,
Evermore your voices raising
To the eternal Three in One.

Come and worship! Come and worship!
Worship Christ the newborn King!

ANGELS WE HAVE HEARD ON HIGH

1. Angels we have heard on high
Sweetly singing o'er the plains,
And the mountains in reply
Echoing their joyous strains.

Gloria in excelsis Deo,
Gloria in excelsis Deo.

2. Shepherds, why this jubilee?
Why your joyous strains prolong?
What the gladsome tidings be
Which inspire your heavenly song?

Gloria in excelsis Deo,
Gloria in excelsis Deo.

3. Come to Bethlehem and see
Him whose birth the angels sing;
Come, adore on bended knee
Christ, the Lord, the new-born King.

Gloria in excelsis Deo,
Gloria, in excelsis Deo.

4. See him in a manger laid
Whom the angels praise above;
Mary, Joseph, lend your aid,
While we raise our hearts in love.

Gloria in excelsis Deo,
Gloria in excelsis Deo.

AWAY IN A MANGER

1. Away in a manger, no crib for a bed,
The little Lord Jesus laid down His sweet head.
The stars in the sky looked down where He lay,
The little Lord Jesus, asleep on the hay.

2. The cattle are lowing, the baby awakes,
But Little Lord Jesus, no crying He makes.
I love Thee, Lord Jesus, look down from the sky,
And stay by my cradle till morning is nigh.

3. Be near me, Lord Jesus; I ask Thee to stay
Close by me forever, and love me, I pray.
Bless all the dear children in Thy tender care,
And fit us for heaven, to live with Thee there.

CAROL OF THE BELLS

Hark to the bells, hark to the bells,
Telling us all Jesus is King!
Strongly they chime, sound with a rhyme,
Christmas is here! Welcome the King.
Hark to the bells, hark to the bells,
This is the day, day of the King!
Peal out the news oer hill and dale,
And 'round the town telling the tale.
Hark to the bells, hark to the bells,
Telling us all Jesus is King!

Come one and all happily sing
Songs of goodwill, o let them sing.

Ring, silv'ry bells, Sing, joyous bells!

Strongly they chime, sound with a rhyme,
Christmas is here, welcome the King!
Hark to the bells, hark to the bells,
Telling us all Jesus is King!

Ring! Ring! Bells.

COVENTRY CAROL

1. Lullay, thou little tiny child
By by, lully, lullay.
Lullay, thou little tiny child,
By by, lully, lullay.

2. O sisters too, how may we do,
For to preserve this day.
This poor youngling for whome we sing.
By by, lully, lullay.

3. Herod the king, in his raging,
Charged he hath this day.
His men of might, in his own sight,
All young children to slay.

4. That woe is me, poor child for thee!
And ever morn and day,
For thy parting neither say nor sing
By by, lully lullay!

THE FIRST NOEL

1. The first noel, the angel did say
Was to certain poor shepherds in fields as they lay;
In fields where they lay keeping their sheep,
On a cold winter's night that was so deep.
Refrain
Noel, noel, noel, noel,
Born is the King of Israel.

2. They looked up and saw a star
Shining in the East, beyond them far;
And to the earth it gave great light,
And so it continued both day and night.
Refrain

3. And by the light of that same star,
Three wise men came for country far;
To seek for a King was their intent,
And to follow the star wherever it went
Refrain

4. This star drew night to the northwest,
O'er Bethlehem it took its rest;
And there it did both stop and stay,
Right over the place where Jesus lay.
Refrain

5. Then entered in those wise men three,
Full reverently upon their knee;
And offered there in His presence,
Their gold, and myrrh, and frankincense.
Refrain

GO TELL IT ON THE MOUNTAIN

1. While shepherds kept their watching
O'er silent flocks by night,
Behold throughout the heavens
There shone a holy light.

Go, tell it on the mountain,
Over the hills and everywhere,
Go, tell it on the mountain
That Jesus Christ is born.

2. The shepherds feared and trembled
When lo! above the earth
Rang out the angel chorus
That hailed our Savior's birth.

Go, tell it on the mountain,
Over the hills and everywhere,
Go, tell it on the mountain
That Jesus Christ is born.

HARK! THE HERALD ANGELS SING

1. Hark! The herald angels sing,
"Glory to the newborn King!
Peace on earth, and mercy mild,
God and sinners reconciled."

Joyful all ye nations rise,
Join the triumph of the skies;
With th'angelic host proclaim,
"Christ is born in Bethlehem."

Hark! The herald angels sing,
"Glory to the newborn King!"

2. Christ, by highest heaven adored,
Christ, the everlasting Lord,
Late in time behold him come,
Offspring of a Virgin's womb.
Veiled in flesh the Godhead see;
Hail, the incarnate Deity,
Pleased as Man with man to dwell,
Jesus, our Immanuel!

Hark! The herald angels sing,
"Glory to the newborn King!"

3. Hail, the heaven-born Prince of Peace!
Hail, the Sun of Righteousness!
Light and life to all he brings,
Risen with healing in his wings.
Mild he lays his glory by,
Born that man no more may die,
Born to raise the sons of earth,
Born to give them second birth.

Hark! The herald angels sing,
"Glory to the newborn King!"

GOOD KING WENCESLAS

1. Good King Wenceslas looked out
On the feast of Stephen
When the snow lay 'round about,
Deep and crisp and even.
Brightly shown the moon that night,
Though the frost was cruel.
When a poor man came in sight,
Gathering winter fuel.

2. "Hither page, and stand by me,
If thou know'st it, telling,
Yonder peasant, who is he?
Where and what his dwelling?"
"Sire, he lives a good league hence,
Underneath the mountain;
Right against the forest fence,
By Saint Agnes' fountain."

3. "Bring me flesh, and bring me wine,
Bring me pine-logs hither;
Thou and I will see him dine
When we bear them thither."
Page and monarch forth they went,
Forth they went together;
Through the rude winds wild lament:
And the bitter weather.

4. "Sire, the night is darker now,
And the wind blows stronger;
Fails my heart, I know not how,
I can go not longer."
"Mark my footsteps, my good page,
Tread thou in them boldly:
Thou shalt find the winter's rage
Freeze thy blood less coldly."

5. In his master's steps he trod,
Where the snow lay dinted;
Heat was in the very sod
Which the saint had printed.
Therefore, Christian men, be sure,
Wealth or rank possessing,
Ye who now will bless the poor,
Shall yourselves find blessing.

IT CAME UPON THE MIDNIGHT CLEAR

1. It came upon the midnight clear,
That glorious song of old,
From angels bending near the earth
To touch their harps of gold.

Peace on the earth, good will to men
From heaven's all gracious King!

The world in solemn stillness lay
To hear the angels sing.

2. Still through the cloven they come,
With peaceful wings unfurled
And still their heavenly music floats
O'er all the weary world;
Above its sad and lowly plains
They bend on hovering wing,
And ever o'er its Babel sounds
The blessed angels sing.

3. Yet with the woes of sin and strife
The world hath suffered long;
Beneath the angel-strain have rolled
Two thousand years of wrong;
And man, at war with man, hears not
The love song which they bring:
O hush the noise, ye men of strife,
And hear the angels sing.

4. And ye, beneath life's crushing load,
Whose forms are bending low,
Who toil along the climbing way
With painful steps and slow:
Look now! for glad and golden hours
Come swiftly on the wing;
O rest beside the weary road,
And hear the angels sing.

5. For lo! the days are hastening on,
By prophet-bards foretold,
When, with the ever-circling years,
Shall come the Age of Gold;
When peace shall over all the earth
Its heavenly splendors fling,
And all the world give back the song
Which now the angels sing.

JOY TO THE WORLD

1. Joy to the world, the Lord
   is come:
   Let earth receive her King;
   Let every heart prepare Him room,
   And heaven and nature sing,
   And heaven and nature sing,
   And heaven and heaven and
   nature sing.
2. He rules the world with truth and grace,
   And makes the nations prove
   The glories of His righteousness,
   And wonders of His love,
   And wonders of His love,
   And wonders, wonders of His love.
3. No more let sins and sorrows grow,
   Nor thorns infest the ground;
   He comes to make his blessings flow
   Far as the curse is found.
   Far as the curse is found
   Far as far as the curse is found.
4. He rules the world with truth and grace,
   And makes the nations prove
   The glories of his righteousness,
   And wonders of His love.
   And wonders of His love
   And wonders, wonders of His love.

O COME, ALL YE FAITHFUL

1. O come, all ye faithful, joyful
   and triumphant,
   O come ye, O come ye to Bethlehem;
   Come and behold Him, born the
   King of angels;
   Refrain
   O come, let us adore Him,
   O come, let us adore Him,
   O come, let us adore Him, Christ
   the Lord!
2. O sing choirs of angels, sing in exultation,
   O sing all ye citizens of heaven above.
   Glory to God in the highest;
   Refrain
3. Sing, choirs of angels, sing in exultation,
   Sing, all ye citizens of heaven above!
   Glory to God in the highest:
   Refrain
4. Yea, Lord, we greet thee, born this
   happy morning,
   Jesus, to thee be glory given;
   Word of the Father, now in flesh
   appearing:
   Refrain

NOEL! NOEL!

1. Noel! Noel! Good news I tell,
   And eke a wonder story:
   A virgin mild hath borne a child,
   Jesus the King of glory.

O COME, O COME IMMANUEL

1. O come, O come Immanuel,
   And ransom captive Israel,
   That mourns in lonely exile here
   Until the Son of God appear.

   Rejoice, rejoice! Immanuel
   Shall come to Thee, O Israel!
2. O come, Thou Key of David, come
   And open wide our heav'nly home.
   Make safe the way that leads on high
   And close the path to misery.

   Rejoice, rejoice! Immanuel
   Shall come to Thee, O Israel!
3. O come, thou Rod of Jesse, free
   Thine own from Satan's tyranny;
   From depths of hell thy people save,
   And give them victory o'er the grave.

   Rejoice, rejoice! Immanuel
   Shall come to thee, O Israel.
4. O come, thou Dayspring, come
   and cheer
   Our spirits by thine advent here;
   Disperse the gloomy clouds of night,
   And death's dark shadows put to flight.

   Rejoice, rejoice! Immanuel
   Shall come to thee, O Israel.
5. O come, thou Key of David, come,
   And open wide our heavenly home;
   Make safe the way that leads on high,
   And close the path to misery.

   Rejoice, rejoice! Immanuel
   Shall come to thee, O Israel.

O LITTLE TOWN OF BETHLEHEM

1. O Little Town of Bethlehem,
   How still we see thee lie!
   Above thy deep and dreamless sleep
   The silent stars go by;
   Yet in thy dark streets shineth
   The everlasting light;
   The hopes and fears of all the years
   Are met in thee tonight.
2. Christ is born of Mary,
   And gathered all above,
   While mortals sleep the angels keep
   Their watch of wond'ring love.
   O morning stars, together
   Proclaim the holy birth!
   And praises sing to God the King,
   And peace to men on earth!
3. How silently, how silently,
   The wondrous Gift is given!
   So God imparts to human hearts
   The blessings of his heaven.
   No ear may hear his coming,
   But in this world of sin,
   Where meek souls will receive
   Him, still
   The dear Christ enters in.
4. O holy Child of Bethlehem,
   Descend to us, we pray;
   Cast out our sin, and enter in,
   Be born in us today.
   We hear the Christmas angels
   The great glad tidings tell;
   O come to us, abide with us,
   Our Lord Immanuel!

O HOLY NIGHT

1. O holy night the stars are
   brightly shining,
   It is the night of the dear Savior's birth;
   Long lay the world in sin and
   error pining,
   Till He appeared and the soul felt
   its worth.

   A thrill of hope the weary soul rejoices,
   For yonder breaks a new and
   glorious morn;

   Fall on your knees, oh, hear the
   angel voices!
   O night divine, o night when Christ
   was born!
   O night, o holy night, o night divine!

2. Truly He taught us to love
   one another,
   His law is love, and His gospel is peace;
   Chains shall He break for the slave is
   our brother,
   And in His name all oppression
   shall cease.

   Sweet hymns of joy in grateful chorus
   raise we,
   Let all within us praise His holy name;

   Christ is the Lord, oh, praise His
   name forever!
   His pow'r and glory ever more proclaim!
   His pow'r and glory evermore proclaim!

SILENT NIGHT

1. Silent night, holy night!
   All is calm, all is bright.
   Round yon Virgin Mother and child.
   Holy infant so tender and mild,
   Sleep in heavenly peace,
   Sleep in heavenly peace.

2. Silent night, holy night!
   Shepherds quake at the sight.
   Glories stream from heaven afar
   Heavenly hosts sing Alleluia,
   Christ the Savior is born!
   Christ the Savior is born

3. Silent night, holy night!
   Son of God love's pure light.
   Radiant beams from thy holy face
   With the dawn of redeeming grace,
   Jesus Lord, at Thy birth.
   Jesus Lord at Thy birth.

WE THREE KINGS OF ORIENT ARE

1. We three Kings of Orient are;
   Bearing gifts we traverse afar,
   Field and fountain, moor
   and mountain,
   Following yonder star. O...
   Refrain
   Star of wonder, star of night,
   Star with royal beauty bright,
   Westward leading, still proceeding,
   Guide us to thy perfect light.

2. Born a King on Bethlehem plain,
   Gold I bring to crown him again,
   King forever, ceasing never,
   Over us all to reign.
   Refrain

3. Frankincense to offer have I;
   Incense owns a Deity nigh;
   Prayer and praising, all men raising,
   Worship Him, God most high.
   Refrain

4. Myrrh is mine: it's bitter perfume
   Breathes a life of gathering gloom:
   Sorrowing, sighing, bleeding, dying;
   Sealed in the stone-cold tomb.
   Refrain

5. Glorious now, behold Him arise,
   King and God, and Sacrifice!
   Heav'n sings alleluya,
   Alleluya the earth replies:
   Refrain

WHAT CHILD IS THIS?

1. What child is this, who, laid to rest,
   On Mary's lap is sleeping?
   Whom angels greet with anthems sweet
   While shepherds watch are keeping?

   This, this is Christ the King,
   Whom shepherds guard and angels sing;
   Haste, haste to bring him laud,
   The babe, the son of Mary.

2. So bring Him incense, gold and myrrh,
   Come peasant King to own Him;
   The Kings of kings salvation brings,
   Let loving hearts enthrone Him.

   Raise, raise the song on high,
   The Virgin sings her lullaby:
   Joy, joy for Christ is born,
   The babe, the son of Mary.

JOY TO THE WORLD

1. Joy to the world, the Lord
   is come:
   Let earth receive her King;
   Let every heart prepare Him room,
   And heaven and nature sing,
   And heaven and nature sing,
   And heaven and heaven and
   nature sing.

2. He rules the world with truth and grace,
   And makes the nations prove
   The glories of His righteousness,
   And wonders of His love,
   And wonders of His love,
   And wonders, wonders of His love.

3. No more let sins and sorrows grow,
   Nor thorns infest the ground;
   He comes to make his blessings flow
   Far as the curse is found.
   Far as the curse is found
   Far as far as the curse is found.

4. He rules the world with truth and grace,
   And makes the nations prove
   The glories of his righteousness,
   And wonders of His love.
   And wonders of His love
   And wonders, wonders of His love.

O COME, ALL YE FAITHFUL

1. O come, all ye faithful, joyful
   and triumphant,
   O come ye, O come ye to Bethlehem;
   Come and behold Him, born the
   King of angels;
   Refrain
   O come, let us adore Him,
   O come, let us adore Him,
   O come, let us adore Him, Christ
   the Lord!

2. O sing choirs of angels, sing in exultation,
   O sing all ye citizens of heaven above.
   Glory to God in the highest;
   Refrain

3. Sing, choirs of angels, sing in exultation,
   Sing, all ye citizens of heaven above!
   Glory to God in the highest:
   Refrain

4. Yea, Lord, we greet thee, born this
   happy morning,
   Jesus, to thee be glory given;
   Word of the Father, now in flesh
   appearing:
   Refrain

NOEL! NOEL!

1. Noel! Noel! Good news I tell,
   And eke a wonder story:
   A virgin mild hath borne a child,
   Jesus the King of glory.

O COME, O COME IMMANUEL

1. O come, O come Immanuel,
   And ransom captive Israel,
   That mourns in lonely exile here
   Until the Son of God appear.

   Rejoice, rejoice! Immanuel
   Shall come to Thee, O Israel!

2. O come, Thou Key of David, come
   And open wide our heav'nly home.
   Make safe the way that leads on high
   And close the path to misery.

   Rejoice, rejoice! Immanuel
   Shall come to Thee, O Israel!

3. O come, thou Rod of Jesse, free
   Thine own from Satan's tyranny;
   From depths of hell thy people save,
   And give them victory o'er the grave.

   Rejoice, rejoice! Immanuel
   Shall come to thee, O Israel.

4. O come, thou Dayspring, come
   and cheer
   Our spirits by thine advent here;
   Disperse the gloomy clouds of night,
   And death's dark shadows put to flight.

   Rejoice, rejoice! Immanuel
   Shall come to thee, O Israel.

5. O come, thou Key of David, come,
   And open wide our heavenly home;
   Make safe the way that leads on high,
   And close the path to misery.

   Rejoice, rejoice! Immanuel
   Shall come to thee, O Israel.

O LITTLE TOWN OF BETHLEHEM

1. O Little Town of Bethlehem,
   How still we see thee lie!
   Above thy deep and dreamless sleep
   The silent stars go by;
   Yet in thy dark streets shineth
   The everlasting light;
   The hopes and fears of all the years
   Are met in thee tonight.

2. Christ is born of Mary,
   And gathered all above,
   While mortals sleep the angels keep
   Their watch of wond'ring love.
   O morning stars, together
   Proclaim the holy birth!
   And praises sing to God the King,
   And peace to men on earth!

3. How silently, how silently,
   The wondrous Gift is given!
   So God imparts to human hearts
   The blessings of his heaven.
   No ear may hear his coming,
   But in this world of sin,
   Where meek souls will receive
   Him, still
   The dear Christ enters in.

4. O holy Child of Bethlehem,
   Descend to us, we pray;
   Cast out our sin, and enter in,
   Be born in us today.
   We hear the Christmas angels
   The great glad tidings tell;
   O come to us, abide with us,
   Our Lord Immanuel!

O HOLY NIGHT

1. O holy night the stars are brightly shining,
It is the night of the dear Savior's birth;
Long lay the world in sin and error pining,
Till He appeared and the soul felt its worth.

A thrill of hope the weary soul rejoices,
For yonder breaks a new and glorious morn;

Fall on your knees, oh, hear the angel voices!
O night divine, o night when Christ was born!
O night, o holy night, o night divine!

2. Truly He taught us to love one another,
His law is love, and His gospel is peace;
Chains shall He break for the slave is our brother,
And in His name all oppression shall cease.

Sweet hymns of joy in grateful chorus raise we,
Let all within us praise His holy name;

Christ is the Lord, oh, praise His name forever!
His pow'r and glory ever more proclaim!
His pow'r and glory evermore proclaim!

SILENT NIGHT

1. Silent night, holy night!
All is calm, all is bright.
Round yon Virgin Mother and child.
Holy infant so tender and mild,
Sleep in heavenly peace,
Sleep in heavenly peace.

2. Silent night, holy night!
Shepherds quake at the sight.
Glories stream from heaven afar
Heavenly hosts sing Alleluia,
Christ the Savior is born!
Christ the Savior is born

3. Silent night, holy night!
Son of God love's pure light.
Radiant beams from thy holy face
With the dawn of redeeming grace,
Jesus Lord, at Thy birth.
Jesus Lord at Thy birth.

WE THREE KINGS OF ORIENT ARE

1. We three Kings of Orient are;
Bearing gifts we traverse afar,
Field and fountain, moor and mountain,
Following yonder star. O...
Refrain
Star of wonder, star of night,
Star with royal beauty bright,
Westward leading, still proceeding,
Guide us to thy perfect light.

2. Born a King on Bethlehem plain,
Gold I bring to crown him again,
King forever, ceasing never,
Over us all to reign.
Refrain

3. Frankincense to offer have I;
Incense owns a Deity nigh;
Prayer and praising, all men raising,
Worship Him, God most high.
Refrain

4. Myrrh is mine: it's bitter perfume
Breathes a life of gathering gloom:
Sorrowing, sighing, bleeding, dying;
Sealed in the stone-cold tomb.
Refrain

5. Glorious now, behold Him arise,
King and God, and Sacrifice!
Heav'n sings alleluya,
Alleluya the earth replies:
Refrain

WHAT CHILD IS THIS?

1. What child is this, who, laid to rest,
On Mary's lap is sleeping?
Whom angels greet with anthems sweet
While shepherds watch are keeping?

This, this is Christ the King,
Whom shepherds guard and angels sing;
Haste, haste to bring him laud,
The babe, the son of Mary.

2. So bring Him incense, gold and myrrh,
Come peasant King to own Him;
The Kings of kings salvation brings,
Let loving hearts enthrone Him.

Raise, raise the song on high,
The Virgin sings her lullaby:
Joy, joy for Christ is born,
The babe, the son of Mary.

JOY TO THE WORLD

1. Joy to the world, the Lord
   is come:
   Let earth receive her King;
   Let every heart prepare Him room,
   And heaven and nature sing,
   And heaven and nature sing,
   And heaven and heaven and
   nature sing.

2. He rules the world with truth and grace,
   And makes the nations prove
   The glories of His righteousness,
   And wonders of His love,
   And wonders of His love,
   And wonders, wonders of His love.

3. No more let sins and sorrows grow,
   Nor thorns infest the ground;
   He comes to make his blessings flow
   Far as the curse is found.
   Far as the curse is found
   Far as far as the curse is found.

4. He rules the world with truth and grace,
   And makes the nations prove
   The glories of his righteousness,
   And wonders of His love.
   And wonders of His love
   And wonders, wonders of His love.

O COME, ALL YE FAITHFUL

1. O come, all ye faithful, joyful
   and triumphant,
   O come ye, O come ye to Bethlehem;
   Come and behold Him, born the
   King of angels;
   Refrain
   O come, let us adore Him,
   O come, let us adore Him,
   O come, let us adore Him, Christ
   the Lord!

2. O sing choirs of angels, sing in exultation,
   O sing all ye citizens of heaven above.
   Glory to God in the highest;
   Refrain

3. Sing, choirs of angels, sing in exultation,
   Sing, all ye citizens of heaven above!
   Glory to God in the highest:
   Refrain

4. Yea, Lord, we greet thee, born this
   happy morning,
   Jesus, to thee be glory given;
   Word of the Father, now in flesh
   appearing:
   Refrain

NOEL! NOEL!

1. Noel! Noel! Good news I tell,
   And eke a wonder story:
   A virgin mild hath borne a child,
   Jesus the King of glory.

O COME, O COME IMMANUEL

1. O come, O come Immanuel,
   And ransom captive Israel,
   That mourns in lonely exile here
   Until the Son of God appear.

   Rejoice, rejoice! Immanuel
   Shall come to Thee, O Israel!

2. O come, Thou Key of David, come
   And open wide our heav'nly home.
   Make safe the way that leads on high
   And close the path to misery.

   Rejoice, rejoice! Immanuel
   Shall come to Thee, O Israel!

3. O come, thou Rod of Jesse, free
   Thine own from Satan's tyranny;
   From depths of hell thy people save,
   And give them victory o'er the grave.

   Rejoice, rejoice! Immanuel
   Shall come to thee, O Israel.

4. O come, thou Dayspring, come
   and cheer
   Our spirits by thine advent here;
   Disperse the gloomy clouds of night,
   And death's dark shadows put to flight.

   Rejoice, rejoice! Immanuel
   Shall come to thee, O Israel.

5. O come, thou Key of David, come,
   And open wide our heavenly home;
   Make safe the way that leads on high,
   And close the path to misery.

   Rejoice, rejoice! Immanuel
   Shall come to thee, O Israel.

O LITTLE TOWN OF BETHLEHEM

1. O Little Town of Bethlehem,
   How still we see thee lie!
   Above thy deep and dreamless sleep
   The silent stars go by;
   Yet in thy dark streets shineth
   The everlasting light;
   The hopes and fears of all the years
   Are met in thee tonight.

2. Christ is born of Mary,
   And gathered all above,
   While mortals sleep the angels keep
   Their watch of wond'ring love.
   O morning stars, together
   Proclaim the holy birth!
   And praises sing to God the King,
   And peace to men on earth!

3. How silently, how silently,
   The wondrous Gift is given!
   So God imparts to human hearts
   The blessings of his heaven.
   No ear may hear his coming,
   But in this world of sin,
   Where meek souls will receive
   Him, still
   The dear Christ enters in.

4. O holy Child of Bethlehem,
   Descend to us, we pray;
   Cast out our sin, and enter in,
   Be born in us today.
   We hear the Christmas angels
   The great glad tidings tell;
   O come to us, abide with us,
   Our Lord Immanuel!

O HOLY NIGHT

1. O holy night the stars are
   brightly shining,
   It is the night of the dear Savior's birth;
   Long lay the world in sin and
   error pining,
   Till He appeared and the soul felt
   its worth.

   A thrill of hope the weary soul rejoices,
   For yonder breaks a new and
   glorious morn;

   Fall on your knees, oh, hear the
   angel voices!
   O night divine, o night when Christ
   was born!
   O night, o holy night, o night divine!

2. Truly He taught us to love
   one another,
   His law is love, and His gospel is peace;
   Chains shall He break for the slave is
   our brother,
   And in His name all oppression
   shall cease.

   Sweet hymns of joy in grateful chorus
   raise we,
   Let all within us praise His holy name;

   Christ is the Lord, oh, praise His
   name forever!
   His pow'r and glory ever more proclaim!
   His pow'r and glory evermore proclaim!

SILENT NIGHT

1. Silent night, holy night!
   All is calm, all is bright.
   Round yon Virgin Mother and child.
   Holy infant so tender and mild,
   Sleep in heavenly peace,
   Sleep in heavenly peace.

2. Silent night, holy night!
   Shepherds quake at the sight.
   Glories stream from heaven afar
   Heavenly hosts sing Alleluia,
   Christ the Savior is born!
   Christ the Savior is born

3. Silent night, holy night!
   Son of God love's pure light.
   Radiant beams from thy holy face
   With the dawn of redeeming grace,
   Jesus Lord, at Thy birth.
   Jesus Lord at Thy birth.

WE THREE KINGS OF ORIENT ARE

1. We three Kings of Orient are;
   Bearing gifts we traverse afar,
   Field and fountain, moor
   and mountain,
   Following yonder star. O...
   Refrain
   Star of wonder, star of night,
   Star with royal beauty bright,
   Westward leading, still proceeding,
   Guide us to thy perfect light.

2. Born a King on Bethlehem plain,
   Gold I bring to crown him again,
   King forever, ceasing never,
   Over us all to reign.
   Refrain

3. Frankincense to offer have I;
   Incense owns a Deity nigh;
   Prayer and praising, all men raising,
   Worship Him, God most high.
   Refrain

4. Myrrh is mine: it's bitter perfume
   Breathes a life of gathering gloom:
   Sorrowing, sighing, bleeding, dying;
   Sealed in the stone-cold tomb.
   Refrain

5. Glorious now, behold Him arise,
   King and God, and Sacrifice!
   Heav'n sings alleluya,
   Alleluya the earth replies:
   Refrain

WHAT CHILD IS THIS?

1. What child is this, who, laid to rest,
   On Mary's lap is sleeping?
   Whom angels greet with anthems sweet
   While shepherds watch are keeping?

   This, this is Christ the King,
   Whom shepherds guard and angels sing;
   Haste, haste to bring him laud,
   The babe, the son of Mary.

2. So bring Him incense, gold and myrrh,
   Come peasant King to own Him;
   The Kings of kings salvation brings,
   Let loving hearts enthrone Him.

   Raise, raise the song on high,
   The Virgin sings her lullaby:
   Joy, joy for Christ is born,
   The babe, the son of Mary.

JOY TO THE WORLD

1. Joy to the world, the Lord
   is come:
   Let earth receive her King;
   Let every heart prepare Him room,
   And heaven and nature sing,
   And heaven and nature sing,
   And heaven and heaven and
   nature sing.
2. He rules the world with truth and grace,
   And makes the nations prove
   The glories of His righteousness,
   And wonders of His love,
   And wonders of His love,
   And wonders, wonders of His love.
3. No more let sins and sorrows grow,
   Nor thorns infest the ground;
   He comes to make his blessings flow
   Far as the curse is found.
   Far as the curse is found
   Far as far as the curse is found.
4. He rules the world with truth and grace,
   And makes the nations prove
   The glories of his righteousness,
   And wonders of His love.
   And wonders of His love
   And wonders, wonders of His love.

O COME, ALL YE FAITHFUL

1. O come, all ye faithful, joyful
   and triumphant,
   O come ye, O come ye to Bethlehem;
   Come and behold Him, born the
   King of angels;
   Refrain
   O come, let us adore Him,
   O come, let us adore Him,
   O come, let us adore Him, Christ
   the Lord!
2. O sing choirs of angels, sing in exultation,
   O sing all ye citizens of heaven above.
   Glory to God in the highest;
   Refrain
3. Sing, choirs of angels, sing in exultation,
   Sing, all ye citizens of heaven above!
   Glory to God in the highest:
   Refrain
4. Yea, Lord, we greet thee, born this
   happy morning,
   Jesus, to thee be glory given;
   Word of the Father, now in flesh
   appearing:
   Refrain

NOEL! NOEL!

1. Noel! Noel! Good news I tell,
   And eke a wonder story:
   A virgin mild hath borne a child,
   Jesus the King of glory.

O COME, O COME IMMANUEL

1. O come, O come Immanuel,
   And ransom captive Israel,
   That mourns in lonely exile here
   Until the Son of God appear.

   Rejoice, rejoice! Immanuel
   Shall come to Thee, O Israel!
2. O come, Thou Key of David, come
   And open wide our heav'nly home.
   Make safe the way that leads on high
   And close the path to misery.

   Rejoice, rejoice! Immanuel
   Shall come to Thee, O Israel!
3. O come, thou Rod of Jesse, free
   Thine own from Satan's tyranny;
   From depths of hell thy people save,
   And give them victory o'er the grave.

   Rejoice, rejoice! Immanuel
   Shall come to thee, O Israel.
4. O come, thou Dayspring, come
   and cheer
   Our spirits by thine advent here;
   Disperse the gloomy clouds of night,
   And death's dark shadows put to flight.

   Rejoice, rejoice! Immanuel
   Shall come to thee, O Israel.
5. O come, thou Key of David, come,
   And open wide our heavenly home;
   Make safe the way that leads on high,
   And close the path to misery.

   Rejoice, rejoice! Immanuel
   Shall come to thee, O Israel.

O LITTLE TOWN OF BETHLEHEM

1. O Little Town of Bethlehem,
   How still we see thee lie!
   Above thy deep and dreamless sleep
   The silent stars go by;
   Yet in thy dark streets shineth
   The everlasting light;
   The hopes and fears of all the years
   Are met in thee tonight.
2. Christ is born of Mary,
   And gathered all above,
   While mortals sleep the angels keep
   Their watch of wond'ring love.
   O morning stars, together
   Proclaim the holy birth!
   And praises sing to God the King,
   And peace to men on earth!
3. How silently, how silently,
   The wondrous Gift is given!
   So God imparts to human hearts
   The blessings of his heaven.
   No ear may hear his coming,
   But in this world of sin,
   Where meek souls will receive
   Him, still
   The dear Christ enters in.
4. O holy Child of Bethlehem,
   Descend to us, we pray;
   Cast out our sin, and enter in,
   Be born in us today.
   We hear the Christmas angels
   The great glad tidings tell;
   O come to us, abide with us,
   Our Lord Immanuel!

O HOLY NIGHT

1. O holy night the stars are
   brightly shining,
   It is the night of the dear Savior's birth;
   Long lay the world in sin and
   error pining,
   Till He appeared and the soul felt
   its worth.

   A thrill of hope the weary soul rejoices,
   For yonder breaks a new and
   glorious morn;

   Fall on your knees, oh, hear the
   angel voices!
   O night divine, o night when Christ
   was born!
   O night, o holy night, o night divine!

2. Truly He taught us to love
   one another,
   His law is love, and His gospel is peace;
   Chains shall He break for the slave is
   our brother,
   And in His name all oppression
   shall cease.

   Sweet hymns of joy in grateful chorus
   raise we,
   Let all within us praise His holy name;

   Christ is the Lord, oh, praise His
   name forever!
   His pow'r and glory ever more proclaim!
   His pow'r and glory evermore proclaim!

SILENT NIGHT

1. Silent night, holy night!
   All is calm, all is bright.
   Round yon Virgin Mother and child.
   Holy infant so tender and mild,
   Sleep in heavenly peace,
   Sleep in heavenly peace.

2. Silent night, holy night!
   Shepherds quake at the sight.
   Glories stream from heaven afar
   Heavenly hosts sing Alleluia,
   Christ the Savior is born!
   Christ the Savior is born

3. Silent night, holy night!
   Son of God love's pure light.
   Radiant beams from thy holy face
   With the dawn of redeeming grace,
   Jesus Lord, at Thy birth.
   Jesus Lord at Thy birth.

WE THREE KINGS OF ORIENT ARE

1. We three Kings of Orient are;
   Bearing gifts we traverse afar,
   Field and fountain, moor
   and mountain,
   Following yonder star. O...
   Refrain
   Star of wonder, star of night,
   Star with royal beauty bright,
   Westward leading, still proceeding,
   Guide us to thy perfect light.

2. Born a King on Bethlehem plain,
   Gold I bring to crown him again,
   King forever, ceasing never,
   Over us all to reign.
   Refrain

3. Frankincense to offer have I;
   Incense owns a Deity nigh;
   Prayer and praising, all men raising,
   Worship Him, God most high.
   Refrain

4. Myrrh is mine: it's bitter perfume
   Breathes a life of gathering gloom:
   Sorrowing, sighing, bleeding, dying;
   Sealed in the stone-cold tomb.
   Refrain

5. Glorious now, behold Him arise,
   King and God, and Sacrifice!
   Heav'n sings alleluya,
   Alleluya the earth replies:
   Refrain

WHAT CHILD IS THIS?

1. What child is this, who, laid to rest,
   On Mary's lap is sleeping?
   Whom angels greet with anthems sweet
   While shepherds watch are keeping?

   This, this is Christ the King,
   Whom shepherds guard and angels sing;
   Haste, haste to bring him laud,
   The babe, the son of Mary.

2. So bring Him incense, gold and myrrh,
   Come peasant King to own Him;
   The Kings of kings salvation brings,
   Let loving hearts enthrone Him.

   Raise, raise the song on high,
   The Virgin sings her lullaby:
   Joy, joy for Christ is born,
   The babe, the son of Mary.

JOY TO THE WORLD

1. Joy to the world, the Lord
   is come:
   Let earth receive her King;
   Let every heart prepare Him room,
   And heaven and nature sing,
   And heaven and nature sing,
   And heaven and heaven and
   nature sing.

2. He rules the world with truth and grace,
   And makes the nations prove
   The glories of His righteousness,
   And wonders of His love,
   And wonders of His love,
   And wonders, wonders of His love.

3. No more let sins and sorrows grow,
   Nor thorns infest the ground;
   He comes to make his blessings flow
   Far as the curse is found.
   Far as the curse is found
   Far as far as the curse is found.

4. He rules the world with truth and grace,
   And makes the nations prove
   The glories of his righteousness,
   And wonders of His love.
   And wonders of His love
   And wonders, wonders of His love.

O COME, ALL YE FAITHFUL

1. O come, all ye faithful, joyful
   and triumphant,
   O come ye, O come ye to Bethlehem;
   Come and behold Him, born the
   King of angels;
   Refrain
   O come, let us adore Him,
   O come, let us adore Him,
   O come, let us adore Him, Christ
   the Lord!

2. O sing choirs of angels, sing in exultation,
   O sing all ye citizens of heaven above.
   Glory to God in the highest;
   Refrain

3. Sing, choirs of angels, sing in exultation,
   Sing, all ye citizens of heaven above!
   Glory to God in the highest:
   Refrain

4. Yea, Lord, we greet thee, born this
   happy morning,
   Jesus, to thee be glory given;
   Word of the Father, now in flesh
   appearing:
   Refrain

NOEL! NOEL!

1. Noel! Noel! Good news I tell,
   And eke a wonder story:
   A virgin mild hath borne a child,
   Jesus the King of glory.

O COME, O COME IMMANUEL

1. O come, O come Immanuel,
   And ransom captive Israel,
   That mourns in lonely exile here
   Until the Son of God appear.

   Rejoice, rejoice! Immanuel
   Shall come to Thee, O Israel!

2. O come, Thou Key of David, come
   And open wide our heav'nly home.
   Make safe the way that leads on high
   And close the path to misery.

   Rejoice, rejoice! Immanuel
   Shall come to Thee, O Israel!

3. O come, thou Rod of Jesse, free
   Thine own from Satan's tyranny;
   From depths of hell thy people save,
   And give them victory o'er the grave.

   Rejoice, rejoice! Immanuel
   Shall come to thee, O Israel.

4. O come, thou Dayspring, come
   and cheer
   Our spirits by thine advent here;
   Disperse the gloomy clouds of night,
   And death's dark shadows put to flight.

   Rejoice, rejoice! Immanuel
   Shall come to thee, O Israel.

5. O come, thou Key of David, come,
   And open wide our heavenly home;
   Make safe the way that leads on high,
   And close the path to misery.

   Rejoice, rejoice! Immanuel
   Shall come to thee, O Israel.

O LITTLE TOWN OF BETHLEHEM

1. O Little Town of Bethlehem,
   How still we see thee lie!
   Above thy deep and dreamless sleep
   The silent stars go by;
   Yet in thy dark streets shineth
   The everlasting light;
   The hopes and fears of all the years
   Are met in thee tonight.

2. Christ is born of Mary,
   And gathered all above,
   While mortals sleep the angels keep
   Their watch of wond'ring love.
   O morning stars, together
   Proclaim the holy birth!
   And praises sing to God the King,
   And peace to men on earth!

3. How silently, how silently,
   The wondrous Gift is given!
   So God imparts to human hearts
   The blessings of his heaven.
   No ear may hear his coming,
   But in this world of sin,
   Where meek souls will receive
   Him, still
   The dear Christ enters in.

4. O holy Child of Bethlehem,
   Descend to us, we pray;
   Cast out our sin, and enter in,
   Be born in us today.
   We hear the Christmas angels
   The great glad tidings tell;
   O come to us, abide with us,
   Our Lord Immanuel!

O HOLY NIGHT

1. O holy night the stars are brightly shining,
It is the night of the dear Savior's birth;
Long lay the world in sin and error pining,
Till He appeared and the soul felt its worth.

A thrill of hope the weary soul rejoices,
For yonder breaks a new and glorious morn;

Fall on your knees, oh, hear the angel voices!
O night divine, o night when Christ was born!
O night, o holy night, o night divine!

2. Truly He taught us to love one another,
His law is love, and His gospel is peace;
Chains shall He break for the slave is our brother,
And in His name all oppression shall cease.

Sweet hymns of joy in grateful chorus raise we,
Let all within us praise His holy name;

Christ is the Lord, oh, praise His name forever!
His pow'r and glory ever more proclaim!
His pow'r and glory evermore proclaim!

SILENT NIGHT

1. Silent night, holy night!
All is calm, all is bright.
Round yon Virgin Mother and child.
Holy infant so tender and mild,
Sleep in heavenly peace,
Sleep in heavenly peace.

2. Silent night, holy night!
Shepherds quake at the sight.
Glories stream from heaven afar
Heavenly hosts sing Alleluia,
Christ the Savior is born!
Christ the Savior is born

3. Silent night, holy night!
Son of God love's pure light.
Radiant beams from thy holy face
With the dawn of redeeming grace,
Jesus Lord, at Thy birth.
Jesus Lord at Thy birth.

WE THREE KINGS OF ORIENT ARE

1. We three Kings of Orient are;
Bearing gifts we traverse afar,
Field and fountain, moor and mountain,
Following yonder star. O . . .
Refrain
Star of wonder, star of night,
Star with royal beauty bright,
Westward leading, still proceeding,
Guide us to thy perfect light.

2. Born a King on Bethlehem plain,
Gold I bring to crown him again,
King forever, ceasing never,
Over us all to reign.
Refrain

3. Frankincense to offer have I;
Incense owns a Deity nigh;
Prayer and praising, all men raising,
Worship Him, God most high.
Refrain

4. Myrrh is mine: it's bitter perfume
Breathes a life of gathering gloom:
Sorrowing, sighing, bleeding, dying;
Sealed in the stone-cold tomb.
Refrain

5. Glorious now, behold Him arise,
King and God, and Sacrifice!
Heav'n sings alleluya,
Alleluya the earth replies:
Refrain

WHAT CHILD IS THIS?

1. What child is this, who, laid to rest,
On Mary's lap is sleeping?
Whom angels greet with anthems sweet
While shepherds watch are keeping?

This, this is Christ the King,
Whom shepherds guard and angels sing;
Haste, haste to bring him laud,
The babe, the son of Mary.

2. So bring Him incense, gold and myrrh,
Come peasant King to own Him;
The Kings of kings salvation brings,
Let loving hearts enthrone Him.

Raise, raise the song on high,
The Virgin sings her lullaby:
Joy, joy for Christ is born,
The babe, the son of Mary.

JOY TO THE WORLD

1. Joy to the world, the Lord
   is come:
   Let earth receive her King;
   Let every heart prepare Him room,
   And heaven and nature sing,
   And heaven and nature sing,
   And heaven and heaven and
   nature sing.
2. He rules the world with truth and grace,
   And makes the nations prove
   The glories of His righteousness,
   And wonders of His love,
   And wonders of His love,
   And wonders, wonders of His love.
3. No more let sins and sorrows grow,
   Nor thorns infest the ground;
   He comes to make his blessings flow
   Far as the curse is found.
   Far as the curse is found
   Far as far as the curse is found.
4. He rules the world with truth and grace,
   And makes the nations prove
   The glories of his righteousness,
   And wonders of His love.
   And wonders of His love
   And wonders, wonders of His love.

O COME, ALL YE FAITHFUL

1. O come, all ye faithful, joyful
   and triumphant,
   O come ye, O come ye to Bethlehem;
   Come and behold Him, born the
   King of angels;
   Refrain
   O come, let us adore Him,
   O come, let us adore Him,
   O come, let us adore Him, Christ
   the Lord!
2. O sing choirs of angels, sing in exultation,
   O sing all ye citizens of heaven above.
   Glory to God in the highest;
   Refrain
3. Sing, choirs of angels, sing in exultation,
   Sing, all ye citizens of heaven above!
   Glory to God in the highest:
   Refrain
4. Yea, Lord, we greet thee, born this
   happy morning,
   Jesus, to thee be glory given;
   Word of the Father, now in flesh
   appearing:
   Refrain

NOEL! NOEL!

1. Noel! Noel! Good news I tell,
   And eke a wonder story:
   A virgin mild hath borne a child,
   Jesus the King of glory.

O COME, O COME IMMANUEL

1. O come, O come Immanuel,
   And ransom captive Israel,
   That mourns in lonely exile here
   Until the Son of God appear.

   Rejoice, rejoice! Immanuel
   Shall come to Thee, O Israel!
2. O come, Thou Key of David, come
   And open wide our heav'nly home.
   Make safe the way that leads on high
   And close the path to misery.

   Rejoice, rejoice! Immanuel
   Shall come to Thee, O Israel!
3. O come, thou Rod of Jesse, free
   Thine own from Satan's tyranny;
   From depths of hell thy people save,
   And give them victory o'er the grave.

   Rejoice, rejoice! Immanuel
   Shall come to thee, O Israel.
4. O come, thou Dayspring, come
   and cheer
   Our spirits by thine advent here;
   Disperse the gloomy clouds of night,
   And death's dark shadows put to flight.

   Rejoice, rejoice! Immanuel
   Shall come to thee, O Israel.
5. O come, thou Key of David, come,
   And open wide our heavenly home;
   Make safe the way that leads on high,
   And close the path to misery.

   Rejoice, rejoice! Immanuel
   Shall come to thee, O Israel.

O LITTLE TOWN OF BETHLEHEM

1. O Little Town of Bethlehem,
   How still we see thee lie!
   Above thy deep and dreamless sleep
   The silent stars go by;
   Yet in thy dark streets shineth
   The everlasting light;
   The hopes and fears of all the years
   Are met in thee tonight.
2. Christ is born of Mary,
   And gathered all above,
   While mortals sleep the angels keep
   Their watch of wond'ring love.
   O morning stars, together
   Proclaim the holy birth!
   And praises sing to God the King,
   And peace to men on earth!
3. How silently, how silently,
   The wondrous Gift is given!
   So God imparts to human hearts
   The blessings of his heaven.
   No ear may hear his coming,
   But in this world of sin,
   Where meek souls will receive
   Him, still
   The dear Christ enters in.
4. O holy Child of Bethlehem,
   Descend to us, we pray;
   Cast out our sin, and enter in,
   Be born in us today.
   We hear the Christmas angels
   The great glad tidings tell;
   O come to us, abide with us,
   Our Lord Immanuel!

O HOLY NIGHT

1. O holy night the stars are
   brightly shining,
   It is the night of the dear Savior's birth;
   Long lay the world in sin and
   error pining,
   Till He appeared and the soul felt
   its worth.

   A thrill of hope the weary soul rejoices,
   For yonder breaks a new and
   glorious morn;

   Fall on your knees, oh, hear the
   angel voices!
   O night divine, o night when Christ
   was born!
   O night, o holy night, o night divine!

2. Truly He taught us to love
   one another,
   His law is love, and His gospel is peace;
   Chains shall He break for the slave is
   our brother,
   And in His name all oppression
   shall cease.

   Sweet hymns of joy in grateful chorus
   raise we,
   Let all within us praise His holy name;

   Christ is the Lord, oh, praise His
   name forever!
   His pow'r and glory ever more proclaim!
   His pow'r and glory evermore proclaim!

SILENT NIGHT

1. Silent night, holy night!
   All is calm, all is bright.
   Round yon Virgin Mother and child.
   Holy infant so tender and mild,
   Sleep in heavenly peace,
   Sleep in heavenly peace.

2. Silent night, holy night!
   Shepherds quake at the sight.
   Glories stream from heaven afar
   Heavenly hosts sing Alleluia,
   Christ the Savior is born!
   Christ the Savior is born

3. Silent night, holy night!
   Son of God love's pure light.
   Radiant beams from thy holy face
   With the dawn of redeeming grace,
   Jesus Lord, at Thy birth.
   Jesus Lord at Thy birth.

WE THREE KINGS OF ORIENT ARE

1. We three Kings of Orient are;
   Bearing gifts we traverse afar,
   Field and fountain, moor
   and mountain,
   Following yonder star. O. . .
   Refrain
   Star of wonder, star of night,
   Star with royal beauty bright,
   Westward leading, still proceeding,
   Guide us to thy perfect light.

2. Born a King on Bethlehem plain,
   Gold I bring to crown him again,
   King forever, ceasing never,
   Over us all to reign.
   Refrain

3. Frankincense to offer have I;
   Incense owns a Deity nigh;
   Prayer and praising, all men raising,
   Worship Him, God most high.
   Refrain

4. Myrrh is mine: it's bitter perfume
   Breathes a life of gathering gloom:
   Sorrowing, sighing, bleeding, dying;
   Sealed in the stone-cold tomb.
   Refrain

5. Glorious now, behold Him arise,
   King and God, and Sacrifice!
   Heav'n sings alleluya,
   Alleluya the earth replies:
   Refrain

WHAT CHILD IS THIS?

1. What child is this, who, laid to rest,
   On Mary's lap is sleeping?
   Whom angels greet with anthems sweet
   While shepherds watch are keeping?

   This, this is Christ the King,
   Whom shepherds guard and angels sing;
   Haste, haste to bring him laud,
   The babe, the son of Mary.

2. So bring Him incense, gold and myrrh,
   Come peasant King to own Him;
   The Kings of kings salvation brings,
   Let loving hearts enthrone Him.

   Raise, raise the song on high,
   The Virgin sings her lullaby:
   Joy, joy for Christ is born,
   The babe, the son of Mary.

JOY TO THE WORLD

1. Joy to the world, the Lord
   is come:
   Let earth receive her King;
   Let every heart prepare Him room,
   And heaven and nature sing,
   And heaven and nature sing,
   And heaven and heaven and
   nature sing.

2. He rules the world with truth and grace,
   And makes the nations prove
   The glories of His righteousness,
   And wonders of His love,
   And wonders of His love,
   And wonders, wonders of His love.

3. No more let sins and sorrows grow,
   Nor thorns infest the ground;
   He comes to make his blessings flow
   Far as the curse is found.
   Far as the curse is found
   Far as far as the curse is found.

4. He rules the world with truth and grace,
   And makes the nations prove
   The glories of his righteousness,
   And wonders of His love.
   And wonders of His love
   And wonders, wonders of His love.

O COME, ALL YE FAITHFUL

1. O come, all ye faithful, joyful
   and triumphant,
   O come ye, O come ye to Bethlehem;
   Come and behold Him, born the
   King of angels;
   Refrain
   O come, let us adore Him,
   O come, let us adore Him,
   O come, let us adore Him, Christ
   the Lord!

2. O sing choirs of angels, sing in exultation,
   O sing all ye citizens of heaven above.
   Glory to God in the highest;
   Refrain

3. Sing, choirs of angels, sing in exultation,
   Sing, all ye citizens of heaven above!
   Glory to God in the highest:
   Refrain

4. Yea, Lord, we greet thee, born this
   happy morning,
   Jesus, to thee be glory given;
   Word of the Father, now in flesh
   appearing:
   Refrain

NOEL! NOEL!

1. Noel! Noel! Good news I tell,
   And eke a wonder story:
   A virgin mild hath borne a child,
   Jesus the King of glory.

O COME, O COME IMMANUEL

1. O come, O come Immanuel,
   And ransom captive Israel,
   That mourns in lonely exile here
   Until the Son of God appear.

   Rejoice, rejoice! Immanuel
   Shall come to Thee, O Israel!

2. O come, Thou Key of David, come
   And open wide our heav'nly home.
   Make safe the way that leads on high
   And close the path to misery.

   Rejoice, rejoice! Immanuel
   Shall come to Thee, O Israel!

3. O come, thou Rod of Jesse, free
   Thine own from Satan's tyranny;
   From depths of hell thy people save,
   And give them victory o'er the grave.

   Rejoice, rejoice! Immanuel
   Shall come to thee, O Israel.

4. O come, thou Dayspring, come
   and cheer
   Our spirits by thine advent here;
   Disperse the gloomy clouds of night,
   And death's dark shadows put to flight.

   Rejoice, rejoice! Immanuel
   Shall come to thee, O Israel.

5. O come, thou Key of David, come,
   And open wide our heavenly home;
   Make safe the way that leads on high,
   And close the path to misery.

   Rejoice, rejoice! Immanuel
   Shall come to thee, O Israel.

O LITTLE TOWN OF BETHLEHEM

1. O Little Town of Bethlehem,
   How still we see thee lie!
   Above thy deep and dreamless sleep
   The silent stars go by;
   Yet in thy dark streets shineth
   The everlasting light;
   The hopes and fears of all the years
   Are met in thee tonight.

2. Christ is born of Mary,
   And gathered all above,
   While mortals sleep the angels keep
   Their watch of wond'ring love.
   O morning stars, together
   Proclaim the holy birth!
   And praises sing to God the King,
   And peace to men on earth!

3. How silently, how silently,
   The wondrous Gift is given!
   So God imparts to human hearts
   The blessings of his heaven.
   No ear may hear his coming,
   But in this world of sin,
   Where meek souls will receive
   Him, still
   The dear Christ enters in.

4. O holy Child of Bethlehem,
   Descend to us, we pray;
   Cast out our sin, and enter in,
   Be born in us today.
   We hear the Christmas angels
   The great glad tidings tell;
   O come to us, abide with us,
   Our Lord Immanuel!

O HOLY NIGHT

1. O holy night the stars are
   brightly shining,
   It is the night of the dear Savior's birth;
   Long lay the world in sin and
   error pining,
   Till He appeared and the soul felt
   its worth.

   A thrill of hope the weary soul rejoices,
   For yonder breaks a new and
   glorious morn;

   Fall on your knees, oh, hear the
   angel voices!
   O night divine, o night when Christ
   was born!
   O night, o holy night, o night divine!

2. Truly He taught us to love
   one another,
   His law is love, and His gospel is peace;
   Chains shall He break for the slave is
   our brother,
   And in His name all oppression
   shall cease.

   Sweet hymns of joy in grateful chorus
   raise we,
   Let all within us praise His holy name;

   Christ is the Lord, oh, praise His
   name forever!
   His pow'r and glory ever more proclaim!
   His pow'r and glory evermore proclaim!

SILENT NIGHT

1. Silent night, holy night!
   All is calm, all is bright.
   Round yon Virgin Mother and child.
   Holy infant so tender and mild,
   Sleep in heavenly peace,
   Sleep in heavenly peace.

2. Silent night, holy night!
   Shepherds quake at the sight.
   Glories stream from heaven afar
   Heavenly hosts sing Alleluia,
   Christ the Savior is born!
   Christ the Savior is born

3. Silent night, holy night!
   Son of God love's pure light.
   Radiant beams from thy holy face
   With the dawn of redeeming grace,
   Jesus Lord, at Thy birth.
   Jesus Lord at Thy birth.

WE THREE KINGS OF ORIENT ARE

1. We three Kings of Orient are;
   Bearing gifts we traverse afar,
   Field and fountain, moor
   and mountain,
   Following yonder star. O...
   Refrain
   Star of wonder, star of night,
   Star with royal beauty bright,
   Westward leading, still proceeding,
   Guide us to thy perfect light.

2. Born a King on Bethlehem plain,
   Gold I bring to crown him again,
   King forever, ceasing never,
   Over us all to reign.
   Refrain

3. Frankincense to offer have I;
   Incense owns a Deity nigh;
   Prayer and praising, all men raising,
   Worship Him, God most high.
   Refrain

4. Myrrh is mine: it's bitter perfume
   Breathes a life of gathering gloom:
   Sorrowing, sighing, bleeding, dying;
   Sealed in the stone-cold tomb.
   Refrain

5. Glorious now, behold Him arise,
   King and God, and Sacrifice!
   Heav'n sings alleluya,
   Alleluya the earth replies:
   Refrain

WHAT CHILD IS THIS?

1. What child is this, who, laid to rest,
   On Mary's lap is sleeping?
   Whom angels greet with anthems sweet
   While shepherds watch are keeping?

   This, this is Christ the King,
   Whom shepherds guard and angels sing;
   Haste, haste to bring him laud,
   The babe, the son of Mary.

2. So bring Him incense, gold and myrrh,
   Come peasant King to own Him;
   The Kings of kings salvation brings,
   Let loving hearts enthrone Him.

   Raise, raise the song on high,
   The Virgin sings her lullaby:
   Joy, joy for Christ is born,
   The babe, the son of Mary.

JOY TO THE WORLD

1. Joy to the world, the Lord
   is come:
   Let earth receive her King;
   Let every heart prepare Him room,
   And heaven and nature sing,
   And heaven and nature sing,
   And heaven and heaven and
   nature sing.

2. He rules the world with truth and grace,
   And makes the nations prove
   The glories of His righteousness,
   And wonders of His love,
   And wonders of His love,
   And wonders, wonders of His love.

3. No more let sins and sorrows grow,
   Nor thorns infest the ground;
   He comes to make his blessings flow
   Far as the curse is found.
   Far as the curse is found
   Far as far as the curse is found.

4. He rules the world with truth and grace,
   And makes the nations prove
   The glories of his righteousness,
   And wonders of His love.
   And wonders of His love
   And wonders, wonders of His love.

O COME, ALL YE FAITHFUL

1. O come, all ye faithful, joyful
   and triumphant,
   O come ye, O come ye to Bethlehem;
   Come and behold Him, born the
   King of angels;
   Refrain
   O come, let us adore Him,
   O come, let us adore Him,
   O come, let us adore Him, Christ
   the Lord!

2. O sing choirs of angels, sing in exultation,
   O sing all ye citizens of heaven above.
   Glory to God in the highest;
   Refrain

3. Sing, choirs of angels, sing in exultation,
   Sing, all ye citizens of heaven above!
   Glory to God in the highest:
   Refrain

4. Yea, Lord, we greet thee, born this
   happy morning,
   Jesus, to thee be glory given;
   Word of the Father, now in flesh
   appearing:
   Refrain

NOEL! NOEL!

1. Noel! Noel! Good news I tell,
   And eke a wonder story:
   A virgin mild hath borne a child,
   Jesus the King of glory.

O COME, O COME IMMANUEL

1. O come, O come Immanuel,
   And ransom captive Israel,
   That mourns in lonely exile here
   Until the Son of God appear.

   Rejoice, rejoice! Immanuel
   Shall come to Thee, O Israel!

2. O come, Thou Key of David, come
   And open wide our heav'nly home.
   Make safe the way that leads on high
   And close the path to misery.

   Rejoice, rejoice! Immanuel
   Shall come to Thee, O Israel!

3. O come, thou Rod of Jesse, free
   Thine own from Satan's tyranny;
   From depths of hell thy people save,
   And give them victory o'er the grave.

   Rejoice, rejoice! Immanuel
   Shall come to thee, O Israel.

4. O come, thou Dayspring, come
   and cheer
   Our spirits by thine advent here;
   Disperse the gloomy clouds of night,
   And death's dark shadows put to flight.

   Rejoice, rejoice! Immanuel
   Shall come to thee, O Israel.

5. O come, thou Key of David, come,
   And open wide our heavenly home;
   Make safe the way that leads on high,
   And close the path to misery.

   Rejoice, rejoice! Immanuel
   Shall come to thee, O Israel.

O LITTLE TOWN OF BETHLEHEM

1. O Little Town of Bethlehem,
   How still we see thee lie!
   Above thy deep and dreamless sleep
   The silent stars go by;
   Yet in thy dark streets shineth
   The everlasting light;
   The hopes and fears of all the years
   Are met in thee tonight.

2. Christ is born of Mary,
   And gathered all above,
   While mortals sleep the angels keep
   Their watch of wond'ring love.
   O morning stars, together
   Proclaim the holy birth!
   And praises sing to God the King,
   And peace to men on earth!

3. How silently, how silently,
   The wondrous Gift is given!
   So God imparts to human hearts
   The blessings of his heaven.
   No ear may hear his coming,
   But in this world of sin,
   Where meek souls will receive
   Him, still
   The dear Christ enters in.

4. O holy Child of Bethlehem,
   Descend to us, we pray;
   Cast out our sin, and enter in,
   Be born in us today.
   We hear the Christmas angels
   The great glad tidings tell;
   O come to us, abide with us,
   Our Lord Immanuel!

O HOLY NIGHT

1. O holy night the stars are
   brightly shining,
   It is the night of the dear Savior's birth;
   Long lay the world in sin and
   error pining,
   Till He appeared and the soul felt
   its worth.

   A thrill of hope the weary soul rejoices,
   For yonder breaks a new and
   glorious morn;

   Fall on your knees, oh, hear the
   angel voices!
   O night divine, o night when Christ
   was born!
   O night, o holy night, o night divine!

2. Truly He taught us to love
   one another,
   His law is love, and His gospel is peace;
   Chains shall He break for the slave is
   our brother,
   And in His name all oppression
   shall cease.

   Sweet hymns of joy in grateful chorus
   raise we,
   Let all within us praise His holy name;

   Christ is the Lord, oh, praise His
   name forever!
   His pow'r and glory ever more proclaim!
   His pow'r and glory evermore proclaim!

SILENT NIGHT

1. Silent night, holy night!
   All is calm, all is bright.
   Round yon Virgin Mother and child.
   Holy infant so tender and mild,
   Sleep in heavenly peace,
   Sleep in heavenly peace.

2. Silent night, holy night!
   Shepherds quake at the sight.
   Glories stream from heaven afar
   Heavenly hosts sing Alleluia,
   Christ the Savior is born!
   Christ the Savior is born

3. Silent night, holy night!
   Son of God love's pure light.
   Radiant beams from thy holy face
   With the dawn of redeeming grace,
   Jesus Lord, at Thy birth.
   Jesus Lord at Thy birth.

WE THREE KINGS OF ORIENT ARE

1. We three Kings of Orient are;
   Bearing gifts we traverse afar,
   Field and fountain, moor
   and mountain,
   Following yonder star. O...
   Refrain
   Star of wonder, star of night,
   Star with royal beauty bright,
   Westward leading, still proceeding,
   Guide us to thy perfect light.

2. Born a King on Bethlehem plain,
   Gold I bring to crown him again,
   King forever, ceasing never,
   Over us all to reign.
   Refrain

3. Frankincense to offer have I;
   Incense owns a Deity nigh;
   Prayer and praising, all men raising,
   Worship Him, God most high.
   Refrain

4. Myrrh is mine: it's bitter perfume
   Breathes a life of gathering gloom:
   Sorrowing, sighing, bleeding, dying;
   Sealed in the stone-cold tomb.
   Refrain

5. Glorious now, behold Him arise,
   King and God, and Sacrifice!
   Heav'n sings alleluya,
   Alleluya the earth replies:
   Refrain

WHAT CHILD IS THIS?

1. What child is this, who, laid to rest,
   On Mary's lap is sleeping?
   Whom angels greet with anthems sweet
   While shepherds watch are keeping?

   This, this is Christ the King,
   Whom shepherds guard and angels sing;
   Haste, haste to bring him laud,
   The babe, the son of Mary.

2. So bring Him incense, gold and myrrh,
   Come peasant King to own Him;
   The Kings of kings salvation brings,
   Let loving hearts enthrone Him.

   Raise, raise the song on high,
   The Virgin sings her lullaby:
   Joy, joy for Christ is born,
   The babe, the son of Mary.

JOY TO THE WORLD

1. Joy to the world, the Lord
   is come:
   Let earth receive her King;
   Let every heart prepare Him room,
   And heaven and nature sing,
   And heaven and nature sing,
   And heaven and heaven and
   nature sing.

2. He rules the world with truth and grace,
   And makes the nations prove
   The glories of His righteousness,
   And wonders of His love,
   And wonders of His love,
   And wonders, wonders of His love.

3. No more let sins and sorrows grow,
   Nor thorns infest the ground;
   He comes to make his blessings flow
   Far as the curse is found.
   Far as the curse is found
   Far as far as the curse is found.

4. He rules the world with truth and grace,
   And makes the nations prove
   The glories of his righteousness,
   And wonders of His love.
   And wonders of His love
   And wonders, wonders of His love.

O COME, ALL YE FAITHFUL

1. O come, all ye faithful, joyful
   and triumphant,
   O come ye, O come ye to Bethlehem;
   Come and behold Him, born the
   King of angels;
   Refrain
   O come, let us adore Him,
   O come, let us adore Him,
   O come, let us adore Him, Christ
   the Lord!

2. O sing choirs of angels, sing in exultation,
   O sing all ye citizens of heaven above.
   Glory to God in the highest;
   Refrain

3. Sing, choirs of angels, sing in exultation,
   Sing, all ye citizens of heaven above!
   Glory to God in the highest:
   Refrain

4. Yea, Lord, we greet thee, born this
   happy morning,
   Jesus, to thee be glory given;
   Word of the Father, now in flesh
   appearing:
   Refrain

NOEL! NOEL!

1. Noel! Noel! Good news I tell,
   And eke a wonder story:
   A virgin mild hath borne a child,
   Jesus the King of glory.

O COME, O COME IMMANUEL

1. O come, O come Immanuel,
   And ransom captive Israel,
   That mourns in lonely exile here
   Until the Son of God appear.

   Rejoice, rejoice! Immanuel
   Shall come to Thee, O Israel!

2. O come, Thou Key of David, come
   And open wide our heav'nly home.
   Make safe the way that leads on high
   And close the path to misery.

   Rejoice, rejoice! Immanuel
   Shall come to Thee, O Israel!

3. O come, thou Rod of Jesse, free
   Thine own from Satan's tyranny;
   From depths of hell thy people save,
   And give them victory o'er the grave.

   Rejoice, rejoice! Immanuel
   Shall come to thee, O Israel.

4. O come, thou Dayspring, come
   and cheer
   Our spirits by thine advent here;
   Disperse the gloomy clouds of night,
   And death's dark shadows put to flight.

   Rejoice, rejoice! Immanuel
   Shall come to thee, O Israel.

5. O come, thou Key of David, come,
   And open wide our heavenly home;
   Make safe the way that leads on high,
   And close the path to misery.

   Rejoice, rejoice! Immanuel
   Shall come to thee, O Israel.

O LITTLE TOWN OF BETHLEHEM

1. O Little Town of Bethlehem,
   How still we see thee lie!
   Above thy deep and dreamless sleep
   The silent stars go by;
   Yet in thy dark streets shineth
   The everlasting light;
   The hopes and fears of all the years
   Are met in thee tonight.

2. Christ is born of Mary,
   And gathered all above,
   While mortals sleep the angels keep
   Their watch of wond'ring love.
   O morning stars, together
   Proclaim the holy birth!
   And praises sing to God the King,
   And peace to men on earth!

3. How silently, how silently,
   The wondrous Gift is given!
   So God imparts to human hearts
   The blessings of his heaven.
   No ear may hear his coming,
   But in this world of sin,
   Where meek souls will receive
   Him, still
   The dear Christ enters in.

4. O holy Child of Bethlehem,
   Descend to us, we pray;
   Cast out our sin, and enter in,
   Be born in us today.
   We hear the Christmas angels
   The great glad tidings tell;
   O come to us, abide with us,
   Our Lord Immanuel!

O HOLY NIGHT

1. O holy night the stars are
   brightly shining,
   It is the night of the dear Savior's birth;
   Long lay the world in sin and
   error pining,
   Till He appeared and the soul felt
   its worth.

   A thrill of hope the weary soul rejoices,
   For yonder breaks a new and
   glorious morn;

   Fall on your knees, oh, hear the
   angel voices!
   O night divine, o night when Christ
   was born!
   O night, o holy night, o night divine!

2. Truly He taught us to love
   one another,
   His law is love, and His gospel is peace;
   Chains shall He break for the slave is
   our brother,
   And in His name all oppression
   shall cease.

   Sweet hymns of joy in grateful chorus
   raise we,
   Let all within us praise His holy name;

   Christ is the Lord, oh, praise His
   name forever!
   His pow'r and glory ever more proclaim!
   His pow'r and glory evermore proclaim!

SILENT NIGHT

1. Silent night, holy night!
   All is calm, all is bright.
   Round yon Virgin Mother and child.
   Holy infant so tender and mild,
   Sleep in heavenly peace,
   Sleep in heavenly peace.

2. Silent night, holy night!
   Shepherds quake at the sight.
   Glories stream from heaven afar
   Heavenly hosts sing Alleluia,
   Christ the Savior is born!
   Christ the Savior is born

3. Silent night, holy night!
   Son of God love's pure light.
   Radiant beams from thy holy face
   With the dawn of redeeming grace,
   Jesus Lord, at Thy birth.
   Jesus Lord at Thy birth.

WE THREE KINGS OF ORIENT ARE

1. We three Kings of Orient are;
   Bearing gifts we traverse afar,
   Field and fountain, moor
   and mountain,
   Following yonder star. O...
   Refrain
   Star of wonder, star of night,
   Star with royal beauty bright,
   Westward leading, still proceeding,
   Guide us to thy perfect light.

2. Born a King on Bethlehem plain,
   Gold I bring to crown him again,
   King forever, ceasing never,
   Over us all to reign.
   Refrain

3. Frankincense to offer have I;
   Incense owns a Deity nigh;
   Prayer and praising, all men raising,
   Worship Him, God most high.
   Refrain

4. Myrrh is mine: it's bitter perfume
   Breathes a life of gathering gloom:
   Sorrowing, sighing, bleeding, dying;
   Sealed in the stone-cold tomb.
   Refrain

5. Glorious now, behold Him arise,
   King and God, and Sacrifice!
   Heav'n sings alleluya,
   Alleluya the earth replies:
   Refrain

WHAT CHILD IS THIS?

1. What child is this, who, laid to rest,
   On Mary's lap is sleeping?
   Whom angels greet with anthems sweet
   While shepherds watch are keeping?

   This, this is Christ the King,
   Whom shepherds guard and angels sing;
   Haste, haste to bring him laud,
   The babe, the son of Mary.

2. So bring Him incense, gold and myrrh,
   Come peasant King to own Him;
   The Kings of kings salvation brings,
   Let loving hearts enthrone Him.

   Raise, raise the song on high,
   The Virgin sings her lullaby:
   Joy, joy for Christ is born,
   The babe, the son of Mary.

JOY TO THE WORLD

1. Joy to the world, the Lord
 is come:
Let earth receive her King;
Let every heart prepare Him room,
And heaven and nature sing,
And heaven and nature sing,
And heaven and heaven and
 nature sing.

2. He rules the world with truth and grace,
And makes the nations prove
The glories of His righteousness,
And wonders of His love,
And wonders of His love,
And wonders, wonders of His love.

3. No more let sins and sorrows grow,
Nor thorns infest the ground;
He comes to make his blessings flow
Far as the curse is found.
Far as the curse is found
Far as far as the curse is found.

4. He rules the world with truth and grace,
And makes the nations prove
The glories of his righteousness,
And wonders of His love.
And wonders of His love
And wonders, wonders of His love.

O COME, ALL YE FAITHFUL

1. O come, all ye faithful, joyful
 and triumphant,
O come ye, O come ye to Bethlehem;
Come and behold Him, born the
 King of angels;
Refrain
O come, let us adore Him,
O come, let us adore Him,
O come, let us adore Him, Christ
 the Lord!

2. O sing choirs of angels, sing in exultation,
O sing all ye citizens of heaven above.
Glory to God in the highest;
Refrain

3. Sing, choirs of angels, sing in exultation,
Sing, all ye citizens of heaven above!
Glory to God in the highest:
Refrain

4. Yea, Lord, we greet thee, born this
 happy morning,
Jesus, to thee be glory given;
Word of the Father, now in flesh
 appearing:
Refrain

NOEL! NOEL!

1. Noel! Noel! Good news I tell,
And eke a wonder story:
A virgin mild hath borne a child,
Jesus the King of glory.

O COME, O COME IMMANUEL

1. O come, O come Immanuel,
And ransom captive Israel,
That mourns in lonely exile here
Until the Son of God appear.

Rejoice, rejoice! Immanuel
Shall come to Thee, O Israel!

2. O come, Thou Key of David, come
And open wide our heav'nly home.
Make safe the way that leads on high
And close the path to misery.

Rejoice, rejoice! Immanuel
Shall come to Thee, O Israel!

3. O come, thou Rod of Jesse, free
Thine own from Satan's tyranny;
From depths of hell thy people save,
And give them victory o'er the grave.

Rejoice, rejoice! Immanuel
Shall come to thee, O Israel.

4. O come, thou Dayspring, come
 and cheer
Our spirits by thine advent here;
Disperse the gloomy clouds of night,
And death's dark shadows put to flight.

Rejoice, rejoice! Immanuel
Shall come to thee, O Israel.

5. O come, thou Key of David, come,
And open wide our heavenly home;
Make safe the way that leads on high,
And close the path to misery.

Rejoice, rejoice! Immanuel
Shall come to thee, O Israel.

O LITTLE TOWN OF BETHLEHEM

1. O Little Town of Bethlehem,
How still we see thee lie!
Above thy deep and dreamless sleep
The silent stars go by;
Yet in thy dark streets shineth
The everlasting light;
The hopes and fears of all the years
Are met in thee tonight.

2. Christ is born of Mary,
And gathered all above,
While mortals sleep the angels keep
Their watch of wond'ring love.
O morning stars, together
Proclaim the holy birth!
And praises sing to God the King,
And peace to men on earth!

3. How silently, how silently,
The wondrous Gift is given!
So God imparts to human hearts
The blessings of his heaven.
No ear may hear his coming,
But in this world of sin,
Where meek souls will receive
 Him, still
The dear Christ enters in.

4. O holy Child of Bethlehem,
Descend to us, we pray;
Cast out our sin, and enter in,
Be born in us today.
We hear the Christmas angels
The great glad tidings tell;
O come to us, abide with us,
Our Lord Immanuel!

O HOLY NIGHT

1. O holy night the stars are
   brightly shining,
   It is the night of the dear Savior's birth;
   Long lay the world in sin and
   error pining,
   Till He appeared and the soul felt
   its worth.

   A thrill of hope the weary soul rejoices,
   For yonder breaks a new and
   glorious morn;

   Fall on your knees, oh, hear the
   angel voices!
   O night divine, o night when Christ
   was born!
   O night, o holy night, o night divine!

2. Truly He taught us to love
   one another,
   His law is love, and His gospel is peace;
   Chains shall He break for the slave is
   our brother,
   And in His name all oppression
   shall cease.

   Sweet hymns of joy in grateful chorus
   raise we,
   Let all within us praise His holy name;

   Christ is the Lord, oh, praise His
   name forever!
   His pow'r and glory ever more proclaim!
   His pow'r and glory evermore proclaim!

SILENT NIGHT

1. Silent night, holy night!
   All is calm, all is bright.
   Round yon Virgin Mother and child.
   Holy infant so tender and mild,
   Sleep in heavenly peace,
   Sleep in heavenly peace.

2. Silent night, holy night!
   Shepherds quake at the sight.
   Glories stream from heaven afar
   Heavenly hosts sing Alleluia,
   Christ the Savior is born!
   Christ the Savior is born

3. Silent night, holy night!
   Son of God love's pure light.
   Radiant beams from thy holy face
   With the dawn of redeeming grace,
   Jesus Lord, at Thy birth.
   Jesus Lord at Thy birth.

WE THREE KINGS OF ORIENT ARE

1. We three Kings of Orient are;
   Bearing gifts we traverse afar,
   Field and fountain, moor
   and mountain,
   Following yonder star. O...
   Refrain
   Star of wonder, star of night,
   Star with royal beauty bright,
   Westward leading, still proceeding,
   Guide us to thy perfect light.

2. Born a King on Bethlehem plain,
   Gold I bring to crown him again,
   King forever, ceasing never,
   Over us all to reign.
   Refrain

3. Frankincense to offer have I;
   Incense owns a Deity nigh;
   Prayer and praising, all men raising,
   Worship Him, God most high.
   Refrain

4. Myrrh is mine: it's bitter perfume
   Breathes a life of gathering gloom:
   Sorrowing, sighing, bleeding, dying;
   Sealed in the stone-cold tomb.
   Refrain

5. Glorious now, behold Him arise,
   King and God, and Sacrifice!
   Heav'n sings alleluya,
   Alleluya the earth replies:
   Refrain

WHAT CHILD IS THIS?

1. What child is this, who, laid to rest,
   On Mary's lap is sleeping?
   Whom angels greet with anthems sweet
   While shepherds watch are keeping?

   This, this is Christ the King,
   Whom shepherds guard and angels sing;
   Haste, haste to bring him laud,
   The babe, the son of Mary.

2. So bring Him incense, gold and myrrh,
   Come peasant King to own Him;
   The Kings of kings salvation brings,
   Let loving hearts enthrone Him.

   Raise, raise the song on high,
   The Virgin sings her lullaby:
   Joy, joy for Christ is born,
   The babe, the son of Mary.

JOY TO THE WORLD

1. Joy to the world, the Lord
   is come:
   Let earth receive her King;
   Let every heart prepare Him room,
   And heaven and nature sing,
   And heaven and nature sing,
   And heaven and heaven and
   nature sing.

2. He rules the world with truth and grace,
   And makes the nations prove
   The glories of His righteousness,
   And wonders of His love,
   And wonders of His love,
   And wonders, wonders of His love.

3. No more let sins and sorrows grow,
   Nor thorns infest the ground;
   He comes to make his blessings flow
   Far as the curse is found.
   Far as the curse is found
   Far as far as the curse is found.

4. He rules the world with truth and grace,
   And makes the nations prove
   The glories of his righteousness,
   And wonders of His love.
   And wonders of His love
   And wonders, wonders of His love.

O COME, ALL YE FAITHFUL

1. O come, all ye faithful, joyful
   and triumphant,
   O come ye, O come ye to Bethlehem;
   Come and behold Him, born the
   King of angels;
   Refrain
   O come, let us adore Him,
   O come, let us adore Him,
   O come, let us adore Him, Christ
   the Lord!

2. O sing choirs of angels, sing in exultation,
   O sing all ye citizens of heaven above.
   Glory to God in the highest;
   Refrain

3. Sing, choirs of angels, sing in exultation,
   Sing, all ye citizens of heaven above!
   Glory to God in the highest:
   Refrain

4. Yea, Lord, we greet thee, born this
   happy morning,
   Jesus, to thee be glory given;
   Word of the Father, now in flesh
   appearing:
   Refrain

NOEL! NOEL!

1. Noel! Noel! Good news I tell,
   And eke a wonder story:
   A virgin mild hath borne a child,
   Jesus the King of glory.

O COME, O COME IMMANUEL

1. O come, O come Immanuel,
   And ransom captive Israel,
   That mourns in lonely exile here
   Until the Son of God appear.

   Rejoice, rejoice! Immanuel
   Shall come to Thee, O Israel!

2. O come, Thou Key of David, come
   And open wide our heav'nly home.
   Make safe the way that leads on high
   And close the path to misery.

   Rejoice, rejoice! Immanuel
   Shall come to Thee, O Israel!

3. O come, thou Rod of Jesse, free
   Thine own from Satan's tyranny;
   From depths of hell thy people save,
   And give them victory o'er the grave.

   Rejoice, rejoice! Immanuel
   Shall come to thee, O Israel.

4. O come, thou Dayspring, come
   and cheer
   Our spirits by thine advent here;
   Disperse the gloomy clouds of night,
   And death's dark shadows put to flight.

   Rejoice, rejoice! Immanuel
   Shall come to thee, O Israel.

5. O come, thou Key of David, come,
   And open wide our heavenly home;
   Make safe the way that leads on high,
   And close the path to misery.

   Rejoice, rejoice! Immanuel
   Shall come to thee, O Israel.

O LITTLE TOWN OF BETHLEHEM

1. O Little Town of Bethlehem,
   How still we see thee lie!
   Above thy deep and dreamless sleep
   The silent stars go by;
   Yet in thy dark streets shineth
   The everlasting light;
   The hopes and fears of all the years
   Are met in thee tonight.

2. Christ is born of Mary,
   And gathered all above,
   While mortals sleep the angels keep
   Their watch of wond'ring love.
   O morning stars, together
   Proclaim the holy birth!
   And praises sing to God the King,
   And peace to men on earth!

3. How silently, how silently,
   The wondrous Gift is given!
   So God imparts to human hearts
   The blessings of his heaven.
   No ear may hear his coming,
   But in this world of sin,
   Where meek souls will receive
   Him, still
   The dear Christ enters in.

4. O holy Child of Bethlehem,
   Descend to us, we pray;
   Cast out our sin, and enter in,
   Be born in us today.
   We hear the Christmas angels
   The great glad tidings tell;
   O come to us, abide with us,
   Our Lord Immanuel!

O HOLY NIGHT

1. O holy night the stars are
   brightly shining,
   It is the night of the dear Savior's birth;
   Long lay the world in sin and
   error pining,
   Till He appeared and the soul felt
   its worth.

   A thrill of hope the weary soul rejoices,
   For yonder breaks a new and
   glorious morn;

   Fall on your knees, oh, hear the
   angel voices!
   O night divine, o night when Christ
   was born!
   O night, o holy night, o night divine!

2. Truly He taught us to love
   one another,
   His law is love, and His gospel is peace;
   Chains shall He break for the slave is
   our brother,
   And in His name all oppression
   shall cease.

   Sweet hymns of joy in grateful chorus
   raise we,
   Let all within us praise His holy name;

   Christ is the Lord, oh, praise His
   name forever!
   His pow'r and glory ever more proclaim!
   His pow'r and glory evermore proclaim!

SILENT NIGHT

1. Silent night, holy night!
   All is calm, all is bright.
   Round yon Virgin Mother and child.
   Holy infant so tender and mild,
   Sleep in heavenly peace,
   Sleep in heavenly peace.

2. Silent night, holy night!
   Shepherds quake at the sight.
   Glories stream from heaven afar
   Heavenly hosts sing Alleluia,
   Christ the Savior is born!
   Christ the Savior is born

3. Silent night, holy night!
   Son of God love's pure light.
   Radiant beams from thy holy face
   With the dawn of redeeming grace,
   Jesus Lord, at Thy birth.
   Jesus Lord at Thy birth.

WE THREE KINGS OF ORIENT ARE

1. We three Kings of Orient are;
   Bearing gifts we traverse afar,
   Field and fountain, moor
   and mountain,
   Following yonder star. O...
   Refrain
   Star of wonder, star of night,
   Star with royal beauty bright,
   Westward leading, still proceeding,
   Guide us to thy perfect light.

2. Born a King on Bethlehem plain,
   Gold I bring to crown him again,
   King forever, ceasing never,
   Over us all to reign.
   Refrain

3. Frankincense to offer have I;
   Incense owns a Deity nigh;
   Prayer and praising, all men raising,
   Worship Him, God most high.
   Refrain

4. Myrrh is mine: it's bitter perfume
   Breathes a life of gathering gloom:
   Sorrowing, sighing, bleeding, dying;
   Sealed in the stone-cold tomb.
   Refrain

5. Glorious now, behold Him arise,
   King and God, and Sacrifice!
   Heav'n sings alleluya,
   Alleluya the earth replies:
   Refrain

WHAT CHILD IS THIS?

1. What child is this, who, laid to rest,
   On Mary's lap is sleeping?
   Whom angels greet with anthems sweet
   While shepherds watch are keeping?

   This, this is Christ the King,
   Whom shepherds guard and angels sing;
   Haste, haste to bring him laud,
   The babe, the son of Mary.

2. So bring Him incense, gold and myrrh,
   Come peasant King to own Him;
   The Kings of kings salvation brings,
   Let loving hearts enthrone Him.

   Raise, raise the song on high,
   The Virgin sings her lullaby:
   Joy, joy for Christ is born,
   The babe, the son of Mary.

JOY TO THE WORLD

1. Joy to the world, the Lord
   is come:
   Let earth receive her King;
   Let every heart prepare Him room,
   And heaven and nature sing,
   And heaven and nature sing,
   And heaven and heaven and
   nature sing.

2. He rules the world with truth and grace,
   And makes the nations prove
   The glories of His righteousness,
   And wonders of His love,
   And wonders of His love,
   And wonders, wonders of His love.

3. No more let sins and sorrows grow,
   Nor thorns infest the ground;
   He comes to make his blessings flow
   Far as the curse is found.
   Far as the curse is found
   Far as far as the curse is found.

4. He rules the world with truth and grace,
   And makes the nations prove
   The glories of his righteousness,
   And wonders of His love.
   And wonders of His love
   And wonders, wonders of His love.

O COME, ALL YE FAITHFUL

1. O come, all ye faithful, joyful
   and triumphant,
   O come ye, O come ye to Bethlehem;
   Come and behold Him, born the
   King of angels;
   Refrain
   O come, let us adore Him,
   O come, let us adore Him,
   O come, let us adore Him, Christ
   the Lord!

2. O sing choirs of angels, sing in exultation,
   O sing all ye citizens of heaven above.
   Glory to God in the highest;
   Refrain

3. Sing, choirs of angels, sing in exultation,
   Sing, all ye citizens of heaven above!
   Glory to God in the highest:
   Refrain

4. Yea, Lord, we greet thee, born this
   happy morning,
   Jesus, to thee be glory given;
   Word of the Father, now in flesh
   appearing:
   Refrain

NOEL! NOEL!

1. Noel! Noel! Good news I tell,
   And eke a wonder story:
   A virgin mild hath borne a child,
   Jesus the King of glory.

O COME, O COME IMMANUEL

1. O come, O come Immanuel,
   And ransom captive Israel,
   That mourns in lonely exile here
   Until the Son of God appear.

   Rejoice, rejoice! Immanuel
   Shall come to Thee, O Israel!

2. O come, Thou Key of David, come
   And open wide our heav'nly home.
   Make safe the way that leads on high
   And close the path to misery.

   Rejoice, rejoice! Immanuel
   Shall come to Thee, O Israel!

3. O come, thou Rod of Jesse, free
   Thine own from Satan's tyranny;
   From depths of hell thy people save,
   And give them victory o'er the grave.

   Rejoice, rejoice! Immanuel
   Shall come to thee, O Israel.

4. O come, thou Dayspring, come
   and cheer
   Our spirits by thine advent here;
   Disperse the gloomy clouds of night,
   And death's dark shadows put to flight.

   Rejoice, rejoice! Immanuel
   Shall come to thee, O Israel.

5. O come, thou Key of David, come,
   And open wide our heavenly home;
   Make safe the way that leads on high,
   And close the path to misery.

   Rejoice, rejoice! Immanuel
   Shall come to thee, O Israel.

O LITTLE TOWN OF BETHLEHEM

1. O Little Town of Bethlehem,
   How still we see thee lie!
   Above thy deep and dreamless sleep
   The silent stars go by;
   Yet in thy dark streets shineth
   The everlasting light;
   The hopes and fears of all the years
   Are met in thee tonight.

2. Christ is born of Mary,
   And gathered all above,
   While mortals sleep the angels keep
   Their watch of wond'ring love.
   O morning stars, together
   Proclaim the holy birth!
   And praises sing to God the King,
   And peace to men on earth!

3. How silently, how silently,
   The wondrous Gift is given!
   So God imparts to human hearts
   The blessings of his heaven.
   No ear may hear his coming,
   But in this world of sin,
   Where meek souls will receive
   Him, still
   The dear Christ enters in.

4. O holy Child of Bethlehem,
   Descend to us, we pray;
   Cast out our sin, and enter in,
   Be born in us today.
   We hear the Christmas angels
   The great glad tidings tell;
   O come to us, abide with us,
   Our Lord Immanuel!

O HOLY NIGHT

1. O holy night the stars are
 brightly shining,
 It is the night of the dear Savior's birth;
 Long lay the world in sin and
 error pining,
 Till He appeared and the soul felt
 its worth.

 A thrill of hope the weary soul rejoices,
 For yonder breaks a new and
 glorious morn;

 Fall on your knees, oh, hear the
 angel voices!
 O night divine, o night when Christ
 was born!
 O night, o holy night, o night divine!

2. Truly He taught us to love
 one another,
 His law is love, and His gospel is peace;
 Chains shall He break for the slave is
 our brother,
 And in His name all oppression
 shall cease.

 Sweet hymns of joy in grateful chorus
 raise we,
 Let all within us praise His holy name;

 Christ is the Lord, oh, praise His
 name forever!
 His pow'r and glory ever more proclaim!
 His pow'r and glory evermore proclaim!

SILENT NIGHT

1. Silent night, holy night!
 All is calm, all is bright.
 Round yon Virgin Mother and child.
 Holy infant so tender and mild,
 Sleep in heavenly peace,
 Sleep in heavenly peace.

2. Silent night, holy night!
 Shepherds quake at the sight.
 Glories stream from heaven afar
 Heavenly hosts sing Alleluia,
 Christ the Savior is born!
 Christ the Savior is born

3. Silent night, holy night!
 Son of God love's pure light.
 Radiant beams from thy holy face
 With the dawn of redeeming grace,
 Jesus Lord, at Thy birth.
 Jesus Lord at Thy birth.

WE THREE KINGS OF ORIENT ARE

1. We three Kings of Orient are;
 Bearing gifts we traverse afar,
 Field and fountain, moor
 and mountain,
 Following yonder star. O. . .
 Refrain
 Star of wonder, star of night,
 Star with royal beauty bright,
 Westward leading, still proceeding,
 Guide us to thy perfect light.

2. Born a King on Bethlehem plain,
 Gold I bring to crown him again,
 King forever, ceasing never,
 Over us all to reign.
 Refrain

3. Frankincense to offer have I;
 Incense owns a Deity nigh;
 Prayer and praising, all men raising,
 Worship Him, God most high.
 Refrain

4. Myrrh is mine: it's bitter perfume
 Breathes a life of gathering gloom:
 Sorrowing, sighing, bleeding, dying;
 Sealed in the stone-cold tomb.
 Refrain

5. Glorious now, behold Him arise,
 King and God, and Sacrifice!
 Heav'n sings alleluya,
 Alleluya the earth replies:
 Refrain

WHAT CHILD IS THIS?

1. What child is this, who, laid to rest,
 On Mary's lap is sleeping?
 Whom angels greet with anthems sweet
 While shepherds watch are keeping?

 This, this is Christ the King,
 Whom shepherds guard and angels sing;
 Haste, haste to bring him laud,
 The babe, the son of Mary.

2. So bring Him incense, gold and myrrh,
 Come peasant King to own Him;
 The Kings of kings salvation brings,
 Let loving hearts enthrone Him.

 Raise, raise the song on high,
 The Virgin sings her lullaby:
 Joy, joy for Christ is born,
 The babe, the son of Mary.

2. Christ, by highest heaven adored,
   Christ, the everlasting Lord,
   Late in time behold him come,
   Offspring of a Virgin's womb.
   Veiled in flesh the Godhead see;
   Hail, the incarnate Deity,
   Pleased as Man with man to dwell,
   Jesus, our Immanuel!

   Hark! The herald angels sing,
   "Glory to the newborn King!"

3. Hail, the heaven-born Prince of Peace!
   Hail, the Sun of Righteousness!
   Light and life to all he brings,
   Risen with healing in his wings.
   Mild he lays his glory by,
   Born that man no more may die,
   Born to raise the sons of earth,
   Born to give them second birth.

   Hark! The herald angels sing,
   "Glory to the newborn King!"

IT CAME UPON THE MIDNIGHT CLEAR

2. Still through the cloven they come,
With peaceful wings unfurled
And still their heavenly music floats
O'er all the weary world;
Above its sad and lowly plains
They bend on hovering wing,
And ever o'er its Babel sounds
The blessed angels sing.

3. Yet with the woes of sin and strife
The world hath suffered long;
Beneath the angel-strain have rolied
Two thousand years of wrong;
And man, at war with man, hears not
The love song which they bring:
O hush the noise, ye men of strife,
And hear the angels sing.

4. And ye, beneath life's crushing load,
Whose forms are bending low,
Who toil along the climbing way
With painful steps and slow:
Look now! for glad and golden hours
Come swiftly on the wing;
O rest beside the weary road,
And hear the angels sing.

5. For lo! the days are hastening on,
By prophet-bards foretold,
When, with the ever-circling years,
Shall come the Age of Gold;
When peace shall over all the earth
Its heavenly splendors fling,
And all the world give back the song
Which now the angels sing.

O COME, ALL YE FAITHFUL

2. O sing choirs of angels, sing in exultation,
O sing all ye citizens of heaven above.
Glory to God in the highest;
Refrain

3. Sing, choirs of angels, sing in exultation,
Sing, all ye citizens of heaven above!
Glory to God in the highest:
Refrain

4. Yea, Lord, we greet thee, born this happy morning,
Jesus, to thee be glory given;
Word of the Father, now in flesh appearing:
Refrain

O COME, O COME IMMANUEL

Semplice

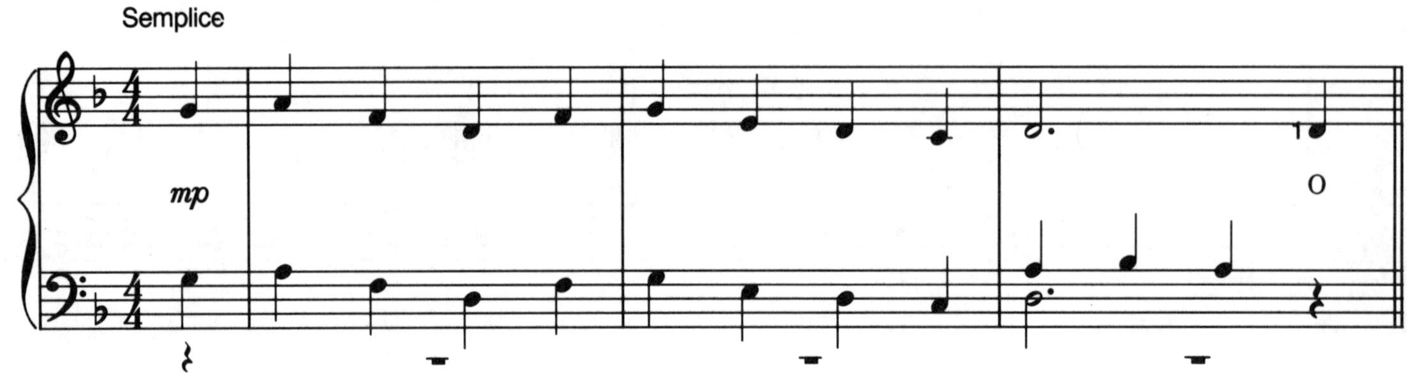

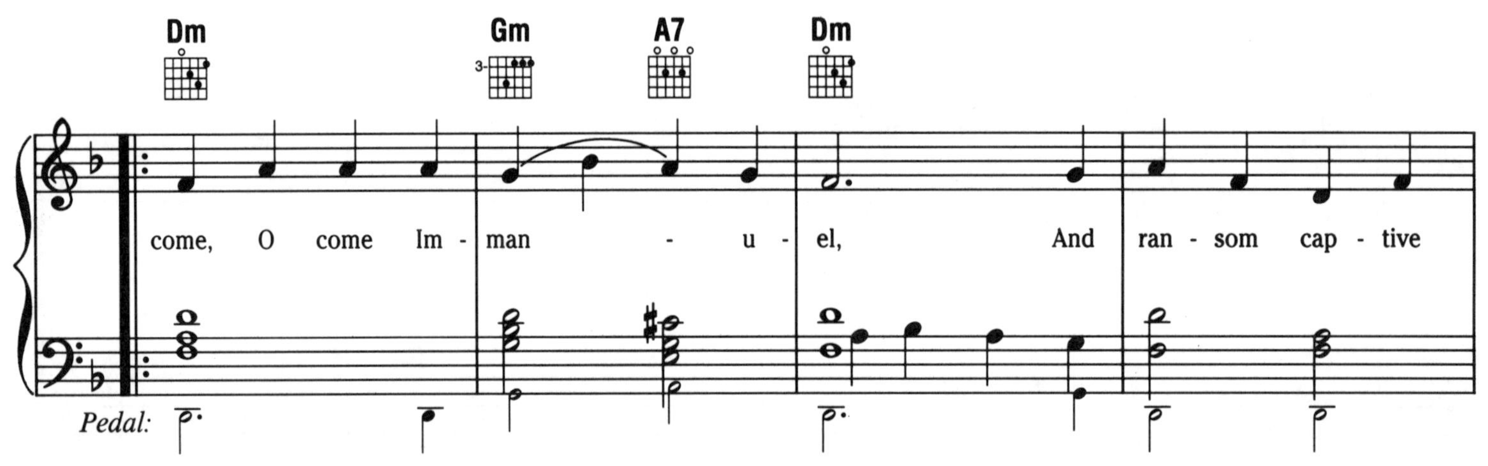

2. O come, Thou Key of David, come
   And open wide our heav'nly home.
   Make safe the way that leads on high
   And close the path to misery.

   Rejoice, rejoice! Immanuel
   Shall come to Thee, O Israel!

3. O come, thou Rod of Jesse, free
   Thine own from Satan's tyranny;
   From depths of hell thy people save,
   And give them victory o'er the grave.

   Rejoice, rejoice! Immanuel
   Shall come to thee, O Israel.

4. O come, thou Dayspring, come
   and cheer
   Our spirits by thine advent here;
   Disperse the gloomy clouds of night,
   And death's dark shadows put to flight.

   Rejoice, rejoice! Immanuel
   Shall come to thee, O Israel.

5. O come, thou Key of David, come,
   And open wide our heavenly home;
   Make safe the way that leads on high,
   And close the path to misery.

   Rejoice, rejoice! Immanuel
   Shall come to thee, O Israel.

O LITTLE TOWN OF BETHLEHEM

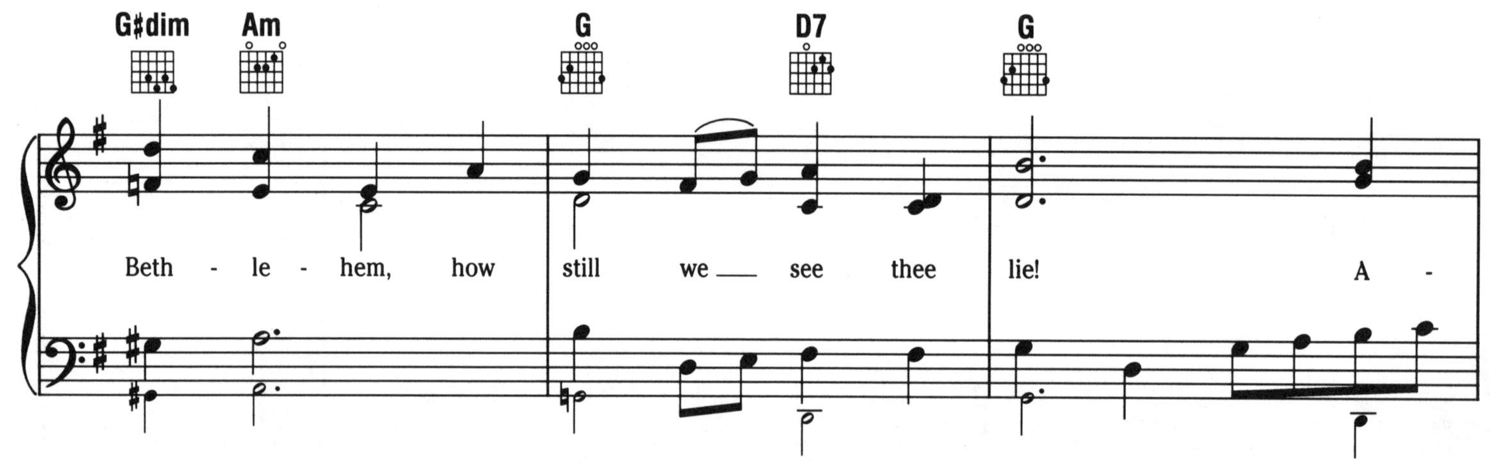

2. Christ is born of Mary,
And gathered all above,
While mortals sleep the angels keep
Their watch of wond'ring love.
O morning stars, together
Proclaim the holy birth!
And praises sing to God the King,
And peace to men on earth!

3. How silently, how silently,
The wondrous Gift is given!
So God imparts to human hearts
The blessings of his heaven.
No ear may hear his coming,
But in this world of sin,
Where meek souls will receive
Him, still
The dear Christ enters in.

4. O holy Child of Bethlehem,
Descend to us, we pray;
Cast out our sin, and enter in,
Be born in us today.
We hear the Christmas angels
The great glad tidings tell;
O come to us, abide with us,
Our Lord Immanuel!

SILENT NIGHT

2. Silent night, holy night!
Shepherds quake at the sight.
Glories stream from heaven afar
Heavenly hosts sing Alleluia,
Christ the Savior is born!
Christ the Savior is born

3. Silent night, holy night!
Son of God love's pure light.
Radiant beams from thy holy face
With the dawn of redeeming grace,
Jesus Lord, at Thy birth.
Jesus Lord at Thy birth.

WE THREE KINGS

*May be played one octave lower

2. Born a King on Bethlehem plain,
   Gold I bring to crown him again,
   King forever, ceasing never,
   Over us all to reign.
   Refrain

3. Frankincense to offer have I;
   Incense owns a Deity nigh;
   Prayer and praising, all men raising,
   Worship Him, God most high.
   Refrain

4. Myrrh is mine: it's bitter perfume
   Breathes a life of gathering gloom:
   Sorrowing, sighing, bleeding, dying;
   Sealed in the stone-cold tomb.
   Refrain

5. Glorious now, behold Him arise,
   King and God, and Sacrifice!
   Heavn'n sings alleluya,
   Alleluya the earth replies:
   Refrain

WHAT CHILD IS THIS?

F E7 Am C
shep - herds watch are keep - ing? This,
lov - ing hearts en - throne Him. Raise,
G Em Am F
this is Christ the King, Whom shep - herds guard and
raise the song on high, The Vir - gin sings her
E7 C G
an - gels sing: Haste, haste to bring him
lul - la - by: Joy, joy for Christ is
Em Am E7 Am
1 2
laud, The babe, the son of Ma - ry. So
born, The babe, the son of Ma - ry.

O HOLY NIGHT

Flowing, with expression
F
p
O ho - ly
Tru - ly He
Pedal:
B♭
F
night the stars are bright - ly shin -
taught us to love one an - oth -
C7
ing, it is the night of the dear Sav - ior's
er, His law is love, and His gos - pel is
F
birth;
peace;
Long lay the
Chains shall He
mf

B♭
F
world in sin and er - ror pin -
break for the slave is our broth -
F7
Am/E
E7/G♯
ing, till He ap - peared and the soul felt its
er, and in His name all op - pres - sion shall
Am
C7
worth. A thrill of
cease. Sweet hymns of
mp
F
hope the wea - ry soul re - joic - es, for
joy in grate - ful cho - rus raise we, let

C7
F
yon - der breaks a new and glo - rious
all with - in us praise His ho - ly
morn;
name;
Dm
Fall on your
Christ is the
f
Am
Gm
knees, oh, hear
Lord, oh, praise
the an - gel voic - es! O
His name for - ev - er! His
ff

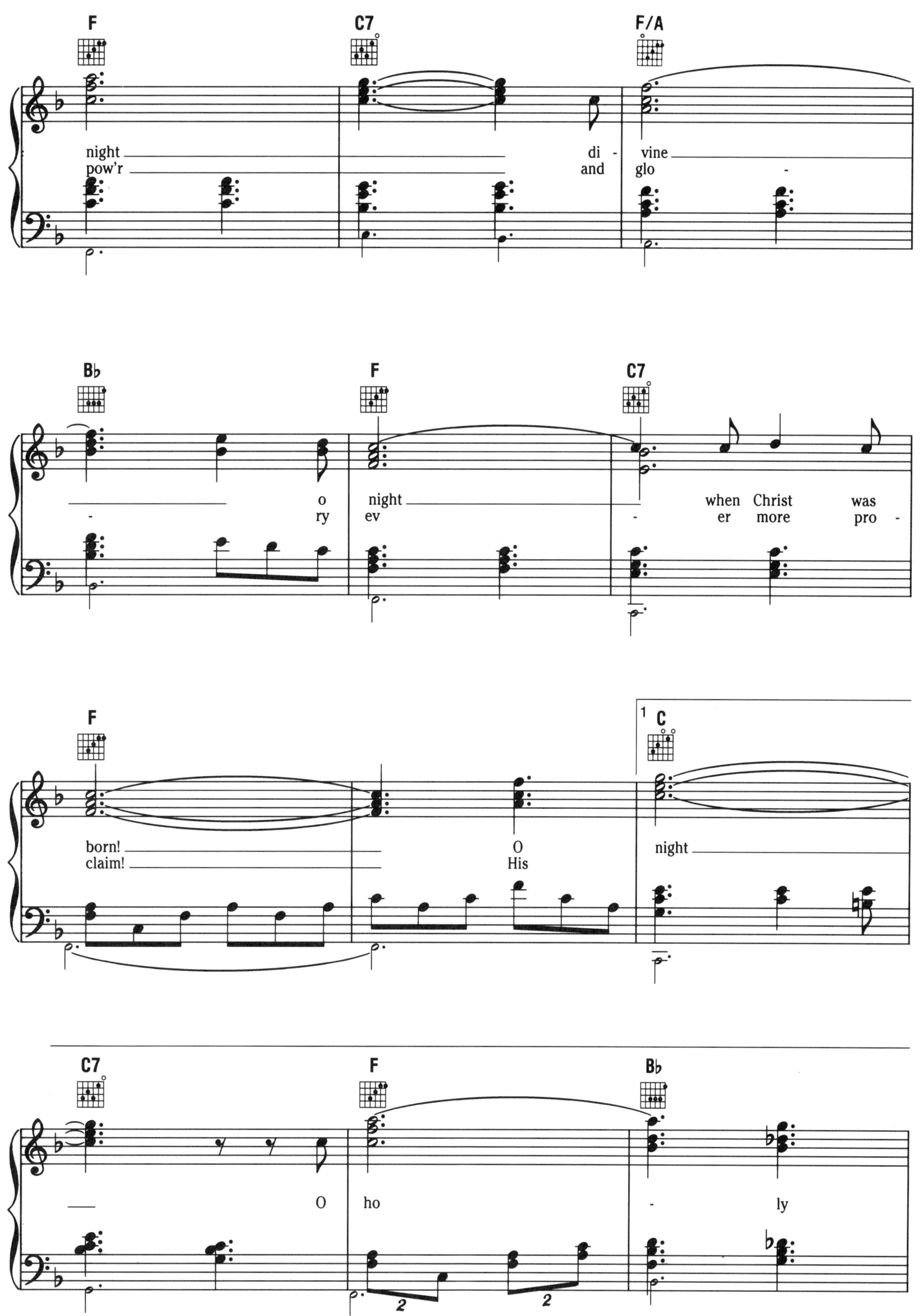
F
C7
F/A
night
pow'r
di-
and
vine
glo-
B♭
F
C7
o
ry
night
ev-
when Christ was
er more pro-
F
1 C
born!
claim!
O
His
night
C7
F
B♭
O
ho-
ly
2
2

F
C7
F
night,
O night di - vine!
2 C
C7
pow'r
and
F/A
B♭
F
C7
glo - ry ev - er - more pro -
F
claim!
dim. poco a poco
pp